DOLPHINS

First published in Great Britain in 1998 by
Colin Baxter Photography Ltd
Grantown-on-Spey
Moray PH26 3NA
Scotland
www.colinbaxter.co.uk

Reprinted 1999, 2000

A CIP Catalogue record for this book is available from the British Library

Worldlife Library Series

ISBN 1-900455-54-4

Photography © 1998 by:

Front cover © François Gohier
Back cover © François Gohier
Page 1 © Roland Seitre (Innerspace Visions)
Page 4 © Tui De Roy (Minden Pictures)
Page 8 © Doug Perrine (Innerspace Visions)
Page 11 © Flip Nicklin (Minden Pictures)
Page 12 © Darryl Torckler (Tony Stone Images)
Page 15 © François Gohier
Page 16 © Phillip Colla (Innerspace Visions)
Page 19 © Michael Nolan (Marine Mammal Images)
Page 20 © François Gohier
Page 23 © James D Watt (Innerspace Visions)
Page 24 © François Gohier
Page 27 © James D Watt (Planet Earth Pictures)
Page 28 © Doug Perrine (Innerspace Visions)
Page 30 © Doug Perrine (Innerspace Visions)
Page 33 © Ben Wilson (Aberdeen University)
Page 34 © Doug Perrine (Innerspace Visions)
Page 37 © Mark Jones (Minden Pictures)
Page 38 © Colour Images Library
Page 41 © Barbara Todd (BBC Natural History Unit)
Page 42 © Stuart Westmorland (Tony Stone Images)
Page 45 © Doug Perrine (Innerspace Visions)
Page 47 © Doug Perrine (Innerspace Visions)

Page 48 © Flip Nicklin (Minden Pictures)
Page 51 © Doug Perrine (Innerspace Visions)
Page 52 © Robert L Pitman (Innerspace Visions)
Page 55 © Michael Newcomer (Marine Mammal Images)
Page 57 © Doug Perrine (Innerspace Visions)
Page 58 © Marc Webber (Earthviews)
Page 60 © Tom Walmsley (BBC Natural History Unit)
Page 63 © Pete Oxford (BBC Natural History Unit)
Page 65 © François Gohier
Page 66 © Doug Perrine (Innerspace Visions)
Page 67 © James D Watt (Earthviews)
Page 68 © Doug Perrine (Innerspace Visions)
Page 71 Top Right © Richard Sears (Earthviews)
Page 71 Top Left © Miguel Iniguez (WDCS)
Page 71 Bottom Right © Richard McLanaghan (IFAW)
Page 71 Bottom Left © Flip Nicklin (Minden Pictures)
Page 72 © Tui De Roy (Minden Pictures)
Page 75 © Lindsay J Porter
Page 76 © François Gohier
Page 79 © Hiroya Minakuchi (Innerspace Visions)
Page 80 © Kate Grellier (Aberdeen University)
Page 83 © Kim Westerskov (Tony Stone Images)
Page 84 © Gregory Ochocki
Page 87 © Gerard Soury (Jacana)

Page 88 © Tony Martin
Page 91 © Fernando Trujillo (WDCS)
Page 92 © Gregory Ochocki
Page 95 © Roland Seitre (Innerspace Visions)
Page 96 © Ravindra Sinha (WDCS)
Page 99 © Mark Carwardine (Innerspace Visions)
Page 100 © Paul Thompson (Aberdeen University)
Page 103 © Steve Dawson (Earthviews)
Page 104 © François Gohier
Page 107 © Ben Wilson
Page 108 © Hiroya Minakuchi (Innerspace Visions)
Page 111 © Doug Perrine (Innerspace Visions)
Page 112 © Doug Perrine (Innerspace Visions)
Page 115 © Ingrid Visser (Earthviews)
Page 116 © Ben Wilson
Page 118 © Kate Grellier (Aberdeen University)
Page 121 Top Right © Ben Wilson (Aberdeen University)
Page 121 Top Left © Sarah Curran (Aberdeen University)
Page 121 Bottom Right © Ben Wilson (Aberdeen University)
Page 121 Bottom Left © Ben Wilson (Aberdeen University)
Page 122 © Barbara Todd (BBC Natural History Unit)
Page 125 © Roland Seitre (Innerspace Visions)
Page 127 © François Gohier

Printed in China

DOLPHINS

Ben Wilson

Colin Baxter Photography, Grantown-on-Spey, Scotland

In memory of Thomas Reid Wilson

Contents

Susu

Spinner

SCALE
1 meter (3.28 feet)

Atlantic Spotted

Franciscana

Commerson's

Peale's

Hector's

Baiji

White-Beaked

Hourglass

Striped

Common

Boto

Risso's

Pacific White-Sided

Chilean

Tucuxi

Dusky

Clymene

Heaviside's

Southern Right
Whale Dolphin

Atlantic White-Sided

Irrawaddy

Rough-Toothed

Fraser's

Pantropical
Spotted

Northern Right
Whale Dolphin

Bhulan

Humpback

Bottlenose

Introduction

The dolphins lord it greatly among the herds of the sea, pluming themselves eminently on their valiance and beauty and their swift speed in the water; for like an arrow they fly through the sea, and fiery and keen is the light which they flash from their eyes, and they descry, I ween, any fish that cowers in a cleft or wraps itself beneath the sands. Even as the eagles are lords among the lightsome birds or lions amid ravenous wild beasts, as serpents are most excellent among reptiles, so are dolphins leaders among the fishes.

Oppianus: *Halieutica* c.AD180

The couple stood at the foot of a shingly Scottish beach, eyes fixed on the water in front of them. Three menacing fins rose, paused, then sank back into the waves. The man stood open mouthed, his wife gripped the corner of his jacket. 'Sharks', he whispered taking another step back from the water's edge. Again the murderous shapes appeared, this time only a few meters from where they stood. Abruptly, the couple's spell was broken by sounds higher up the beach. Swinging round, they saw a Highland terrier scampering towards the water and a man waving a stick back and forth in a throwing motion over his head. As if attached, the dog scurried about, ready to leap into the sea after it. 'Stop, No, Stop', the woman screeched, gesticulating towards the dog walker. As he approached, she stretched out her arm towards the shapes in the waves. 'Look, sharks'. 'Three huge ones, right there', her husband added. The sharks reappeared once again where the stick would have landed. 'See' said the wife. The dog walker stared also. 'Those are the dolphins, they live here'. The couple gawked once more as color returned to their faces, and horror turned to delight. It was at this point that Mr and Mrs Pittman cancelled the remainder of their touring holiday of Scotland to spend the entire fortnight camped at the end of that windy headland to watch the dolphins.

Why do dolphins hold such a special place in our minds? These large aquatic predators bear many similarities to sharks but elicit an entirely different response in us. One might say that it is because dolphins don't eat people, but neither do the majority of sharks and few people want to hear the stories about swimmers who were led into dangerous currents by dolphins or boats that were wrecked while following them. Instead, mythology and modern newspapers alike are peppered with stories of their heroic acts and their consideration for distressed humans, dogs and even horses. Their grinning caricatures are freely littered through our lives, from company logos to postcards, posters and innumerable TV shows. Dolphins, and their allies the whales, as every environmental organization knows, boost subscriptions and media interest like no other animal group. Mass strandings haul reporters out on to distant mud flats while holiday-makers endure enormous journeys and expense to watch or swim with wild dolphins.

Humans are clearly captivated by these animals, but the realities of being a dolphin are often overlooked or grossly oversimplified when they are squeezed into the popular stereotype. How many people realize that there are over thirty very different species, that the color of their skin can include brown, black, yellow, white and pink as well as gray, that they occur not just in the seas and oceans but also live in rivers far inland, and that they provide a living for countless other organisms from bacteria to birds?

The diversity and wonder of dolphins is the substance of this book. In writing it, I have tried to provide a whistle-stop tour rather than an encyclopaedic biology lesson and have focused on those aspects of dolphin life that make them gems of the animal kingdom. A major part of this wonder stems from the large fraction of their lives that still remains unknown. The complexity of the information that they can pass from one to another, whether they can really stun their prey with sound, how they navigate across seemingly featureless oceans, how their societies are composed and maintained and even how many species there actually are, are all poorly understood. However, researchers studying dolphins are becoming armed with an ingenious and sophisticated array of tools to unearth the answers to such questions and with every year dozens of new discoveries are made. Some breakthroughs provide simple answers but the majority give totally unforeseen solutions which themselves spawn new avenues for investigation. Who would have imagined, for example, that the whistling calls that a dolphin will voice when entangled in a net are not simple distress calls but are actually the unique signature of that animal's identity (just like a name) given to it by its mother? Or that their migration paths across oceans may be altered by the movements of atmospheric weather systems, or even that they can live for fifty years and more? As each new discovery is made the complexities of dolphin behavior, ecology and anatomy become more impressive.

The spur for much of the research on dolphins stems directly from concerns for their welfare as many populations, and now several species, are under direct threat of extinction from human activities. In the past, dolphins were widely hunted for food, fishing bait and their oil. Today most hunts have been abandoned, but dolphins now face a profusion of less visible threats that are potentially far more devastating. Oil, pesticide and sewage pollution, overfishing of their prey, entanglement in fishing nets, disturbance, collisions with boats, habitat drainage and dredging make up just the beginnings of a depressing list. It is ironic that at a time in history when dolphins are at their most popular, they face many of the biggest human-related threats to their survival. But conserving dolphins, their prey or their habitats is far from a straightforward process. And as we find out more about how their societies and populations function it has become clear that we still have far to go.

To introduce the dolphins, I have had to cut a genetic corner, because 'dolphins' are not a distinct evolutionary group. Instead, they are all members of a wider collection of about seventy-eight mammal species called the cetaceans, which also includes the whales and porpoises. Like any extended family, some cetacean species are closer relatives than others, but the names whale, dolphin and porpoise do not mark the real boundaries. Bottlenose dolphins, for example, are more closely related to killer whales than they are to the river dolphins. The term 'dolphin' simply separates out the middle-sized members of the cetaceans, with the whales being the big and the porpoises the small ones. But despite their genetically wayward name, dolphins do represent a distinct group, marked out by their lifestyles. All dolphins, unlike many of the whales, chase and eat their prey one by one. To do this they need to be fast and agile and this has led to their distinctive shape and extraordinary swimming skills. Furthermore, their ability to hunt cooperatively and their need to avoid predators has led them to develop complex societies, unrivalled by any species of whale or porpoise.

There are many differences of body form and behavior within the dolphins and most of these, as well as the human threats that they face, result from the habitats they live in. Dolphins can be considered as belonging to three ecological groups; oceanic, coastal and river dolphins. The key to understanding why these groups are different from one another requires an appreciation of what living in each of these surroundings involves. But for us, trying to comprehend these differences requires a huge mental leap. Casting off our land-based attitudes is tough, but imagining a dolphin's world from its perspective is an enlightening experience. My challenge to you is to make this mental leap.

Dolphins, like these two spinner dolphins, hold a special place in the human mind. These high-speed aquatic predators share many similarities with sharks but elicit an entirely different response in us. Perhaps it is their social temperament, intelligence, curiosity and playful nature that, to our eyes, make them such gems of the animal kingdom.

The sleek form that dolphins now sport is a far cry from the four-legged, hoofed stance of their wolf-like ancestors. But deep within modern dolphins are buried mementoes of their past. Their skull bones, kidneys and blood chemistry, for example, are like those of present-day cows, sheep and pigs.

Origins

Whales, dolphins and porpoises collectively belong to a group called the cetaceans (pronounced 'se-TAY-shuns'). They are mammals like ourselves and so belong to the group of four thousand furry, warm-blooded species that includes everything from beavers to bats, lions to llamas. Our common ancestors had humble reptilian beginnings 300 million years ago, way before the rule of the dinosaurs, and only survived their 160-million-year reign of supremacy by staying small and diminutive. As the dinosaurs lumbered into oblivion the mammals evolved rapidly in shape and size to fill the gaps. One pioneering group were hoofed wolf-like predators (the condylarths) that set in train the remarkable evolution of all modern cetaceans. Fossil evidence suggests that about 53 million years ago a long-bodied, thinly furred mammal slipped into a huge tropical lagoon that stretched from modern Spain to the Middle East (the Tethys Sea) and began to pursue fish. This was *Hapalodectes*, looking much like a contemporary otter except that its limbs were hoofed and it was larger, probably 4 ft 6 in (1.3 m) long. Over time, its descendants, like the fossil specimen *Ambulocetus*, became ever more adept at swimming and more vulnerable on land. Propelling itself by beating its tail and trailing legs up and down, it was to set the mould for all modern cetaceans. By 46 million years ago, this line had transformed into *Pakicetus*, a 6 ft 6 in- (2 m-) long creature with nose and eyes high on its head and flippers like those of a modern seal. About 2 million years later, the 10 ft- (3 m-) long *Protocetus* had a massively muscled tail to provide the propulsive force for swimming, and was probably a stranger to land. The aquatic commitment continued and by 35 million years ago all external trace of hind-limbs had gone. Shortly after, there was another explosion of species and most of the modern cetacean groups took the stage.

Colloquially, the modern-day cetaceans are divided into three units by size. The whales are large, dolphins medium and porpoises small but their true evolutionary groupings are not quite so simple. All of the existing cetaceans can be split into two groups. The first is the Mysticeti, which literally means 'mustached whales'. All eleven or so species have no teeth and feed by straining small fish or crustaceans through enormous mouths built like sieves. Their filters are made up of hundreds of plates of a material like thickened fingernail called baleen. Every adult mysticete is big; even the smallest of them is over 19 ft (6 m) in length whilst the largest can be over 100 ft (30 m) and so they are all commonly called whales. The forms found alive today include the fin, humpback, minke, gray and blue whales.

The other group is called the Odontoceti, which literally means 'toothed whales', although it also includes all the dolphins and porpoises: all of the animals in this group have teeth at one stage or another in their lives. There are many more species of odontocetes than mysticetes, at the last count around 65; they come in a wider variety of shapes and sizes and are divided into six families. The Physeteridae includes the largest representative of the odontocetes, the sperm whale, famed for gobbling giant squid in the depths of the ocean and maniacal whalers at the surface. The Ziphiidae or beaked whales are also only found on the high seas, but being more shy are rather mysterious and new ones continue to be discovered. The Monodontidae are a collection of three species that include the Arctic-living narwhal and beluga as well as the first dolphin to appear on our list, the Irrawaddy dolphin. The Platanistidae contains five species of dolphin. Four of them live in rivers, and this group is often called the true river dolphins. The Phocoenidae or porpoises comprise six species, which are all small and include no dolphins.

The final group, Delphinidae, is the stronghold of the species that we commonly call dolphins. There are over 35 species in this group ranging from the rare and tiny Hector's dolphin to the ubiquitous bottlenose dolphin, and from the chubby white-beaked dolphin to the snake-like right whale dolphins. This group also contains the killer, pilot and melon-headed whales.

The exact number of species in each group is far from certain (eleven or so baleen whales, over 35 delphinids and so on) and this is for two reasons. To begin with, the evolutionary boundaries between one species and another are unclear. The traditional test of whether one population of animals belongs to a different species to another population, depends on whether they successfully interbreed between these populations to produce viable offspring. Animals that do share their genetic make-up with one another by interbreeding are considered the same species, but when populations may be separated by thousands or tens of thousands of miles, interbreeding becomes physically impossible. It is inconceivable, for example, that a bottlenose dolphin living off the coast of northern Scotland would mate with a bottlenose dolphin from southern New Zealand. So on this basis could we surmise that the bottlenose dolphins from Scotland and New Zealand belong to different species? Unfortunately not, because whilst these two individuals may never meet, there may be a continuous chain of other bottlenose dolphins between them which may interbreed and so over generations genetic characteristics from the far north may spread to the far south and vice versa. This is not to say that the dolphins at our extremes or anywhere in between need look or behave in an identical fashion to each other because each may have specializations to its local habitats whilst still belonging to the same species.

Imagine that a gap were to appear in the north-south bottlenose dolphin chain, say a change in climate around the equator that produced a rift of a thousand miles over which bottlenose dolphins never crossed. At first, dolphins either side of the gap would be genetically very similar but gradually, over many generations, the north and south populations of dolphins would drift genetically further apart and at some point (perhaps after only a hundred years or over several thousand years) they would become different enough that they could not interbreed given the chance. The evolution of the two species of right whale dolphins (the northern and southern) may be a case just like this.

Now imagine that the climatic conditions that excluded bottlenose dolphins from the equator were relaxed. We would then have outwardly similar bottlenose dolphins continuously from Scotland to New Zealand again, but somewhere in the middle would be an invisible boundary across which breeding could not occur. Thus a simple climatic change operating over hundreds or thousands of years changed one species into two; this is where the problems for the biologists come in.

When we look at the world's bottlenose dolphins there are huge physical and genetical differences between populations in different parts of the world. But it is impossible, at this stage, to tell whether these are simply their adaptations to local conditions or a sign that there is actually no genetic interchange across the populations. 'Lumpers' say that bottlenose dolphins are just one very variable species whilst 'splitters' have defined between three and over 20 distinct species of bottlenose dolphin. Spinner dolphins, humpback dolphins and common dolphins also show similar types of geographical variation.

The second reason why definitions of the number of species of cetacean tend to be rather vague is because we simply know much less about the seas and oceans of the world than is often thought and it is entirely conceivable, likely even, that there are cetacean species living out there that have yet to be documented. After all, all we know about several species of beaked whale comes entirely from the few remains recovered from fish markets or washed up on beaches. How many other species there are out at sea is anybody's guess!

Form and Function

Dolphins spend their whole lives in water. They are conceived there, born there and even sleep there without ever needing to make contact with land. Being freed of a terrestrial base they have exploited all of the great ocean's, most of the seas and several great river systems across the globe. To do this these mammals must not only survive in the water but must beat the existing competition. In doing so, evolution has shaped dolphins, like the whales, to look more like fish than their land-bound forbears, but their mammalian origin has given them a legacy that includes some unexpected advantages as aquatic predators.

Although dolphins are dwarfed by the whales, compared to land mammals they are really quite large. An adult male Risso's dolphin may reach 12 ft 6 in (3.8 m) long and weigh 1100 lb (500 kg); or, to put it another way, is the length of an average car and more than twice the weight of a fully grown lion. Even the smallest dolphin, the tucuxi, reaches 5 ft 3 in (1.6 m) and around 88 lb (40 kg), the length of a bath tub and weight of a fully grown Rottweiler dog. Being big in the sea confers several advantages. For warm-blooded creatures, heat loss is almost always a problem, but this is diminished when the body gets larger. The reason behind this is because big bodies have proportionally less surface area to their volume than small ones. Similarly, the drag when swimming through water on a big animal is proportionally less too. So big means warm and fast but it also gives the potential to have reserves. Fat reserves can provide energy in lean times and oxygen reserves can make long dives routine. It is no surprise, then, that of the cetaceans, the big whales hold the records for the fastest prolonged swimming speeds, longest fasts and deepest dives. But there are, of course, costs in being big. A huge body needs lots of maintenance and so is a burden where food is always scarce. Bulk also limits

maneuverability, explaining why there are no 'river whales'. But even in the bountiful open sea, a big body may be a limitation. The great whales (including the blue, fin, humpback and right whales) all feed on small schooling fish, crustaceans or plankton, which they gulp *en masse*. But a tremendous variety of fish and squid don't swarm like this and so are out of reach for the great whales. A gap in the market exists for fast-swimming predators that are agile enough to pursue their prey one by one. This is where the dolphins and porpoises carve out a living.

Living Torpedoes

To travel at high speeds in water imposes tremendous constraints on the shape that a dolphin can be. The most efficient shape is that of a polished torpedo and whilst several species, particularly the right whale dolphins, have come very close to attaining it they, like all dolphins, must perform other functions. For a start, no dolphin can swim continuously in a straight line but needs to steer. At high velocities, adjustments are made with the pectoral flippers which jut out on either side of the body behind the head. These modified ancestral front limbs are held into the flow and can be delicately tipped forwards and back, like ailerons. At slower speeds adjustments in direction are made by bending the whole body. The fastest swimming dolphins, such as the striped and common dolphins, move around more like bullets than mammals and have small pectoral flippers and stiff bodies. More ponderous swimmers like the river dolphins have big flippers shaped like canoe paddles and a flexible build.

For all dolphins, propulsion comes only from the tail flukes which are pumped up and down by huge muscle masses stretching right along the dolphin's back (dorsal) and from the belly to the base of the tail (ventral). Together, these muscle masses make up about a third of the dolphin's total weight. When the dorsal muscles contract the tail is pulled upwards and produces the forward thrust. Contraction of the ventral muscles forms the downward stroke and brings the tail back to position for the next beat. In all dolphins, the tail-flukes are crescent-shaped blades extending sideways from the very end of the backbone. Surprisingly, the fastest-swimming species have the smallest tail flukes, which they beat over a narrow range and at great speed and the slower-moving dolphins beat their broad flukes over a much wider ark.

The up-down motion of the tail clearly distinguishes the cetaceans from the fish and is only made possible by their flexible back-bone which they owe to their terrestrial ancestors. The first creatures on land had backbones that only flexed from side to side and so walked by swinging the front and back of their bodies to and fro, just like crocodiles do today. But as the land animals became more fleet of foot, a bounding gait took over from the waddling one and required a spine that flexed up and down. This movement becomes very obvious if you watch slow-motion film of a cheetah or a dog running or if you have the misfortune to ride a camel. The supple articulation has been retained by the dolphins and now allows them to dart up or down in the water very easily. Because fish can only beat their tails from side to side they cannot flex up and down and so most can only change depth gradually. So in a chase between a dolphin and a fleeing fish, the dolphin can easily outwit the fish by forcing it to swim up or down. Furthermore, for dolphins, being able to move up and down makes breathing at the surface a smooth and rapid affair. It seems strange to think that galloping around on land for several million years could come in so useful later on in the sea.

Most dolphins, like the rest of the cetaceans, have a dorsal fin. It is formed from tough fibrous connective tissue and contains no bones. Situated at the top of the back, it functions like the keel on a boat and stops the animal from pirouetting in the water. In most species, dorsal fins are falcate (shaped like swept back half crescents) but in several spinner dolphin populations they are tilted forwards rather than back. In some small dolphins, like the Heaviside's, they are triangular and in others like the Hector's and Commerson's they are rounded like one of Mickey Mouse's ears. The right whale dolphins and several river dolphins have lost their dorsal fins altogether and for them pirouetting underwater must somehow be useful.

Except for a few sensory bristles around the snout, dolphins, like all of the other cetaceans, have lost all traces of hair. Genitals and nipples are tucked away inside folds in the skin which itself is smooth and taut like the surface of a boiled egg. This cuts down on the friction of flowing water and denies a foothold for barnacles and other fouling organisms. Below this rubbery exterior is a layer of blubber, made from fibrous tissues and oils. It acts as a heat insulator and fat store and streamlines the body by smoothing out any lumps or bumps from the ribs, vertebrae or skull. Being lighter than water, the blubber also reduces the overall density of the dolphin, giving it more or less neutral buoyancy and so the dolphin need expend no energy in staying at a particular depth in the water.

The streamlined shape, swept back flippers, fin, flukes, massive muscles, slippery skin, and blubber all make dolphins highly maneuverable and capable of some astonishing speeds. Wild dolphins cruise at speeds of around $4\frac{1}{2}$ mph (7 kph) and can lay on short bursts of up to 25 mph (40 kph). Some fantastic velocities, including one at 34 mph (55 kph), have also been reported, but are probably exaggerations or the result of dolphins riding the pressure waves of big swells or the bow-wave of the observers' boat.

Whatever speeds dolphins can truly attain, they are clearly supremely efficient swimmers. It has been calculated that a bottlenose dolphin could swim side by side with our best

Like splinters from Mercury himself, a school of common dolphins tears across the sea's surface at dusk.
These inhabitants of warm seas use currents like the Gulf Stream to migrate into higher latitudes during the summer.
By swimming in formation, each dolphin can ride the slipstream of its neighbor and so travel with great efficiency.

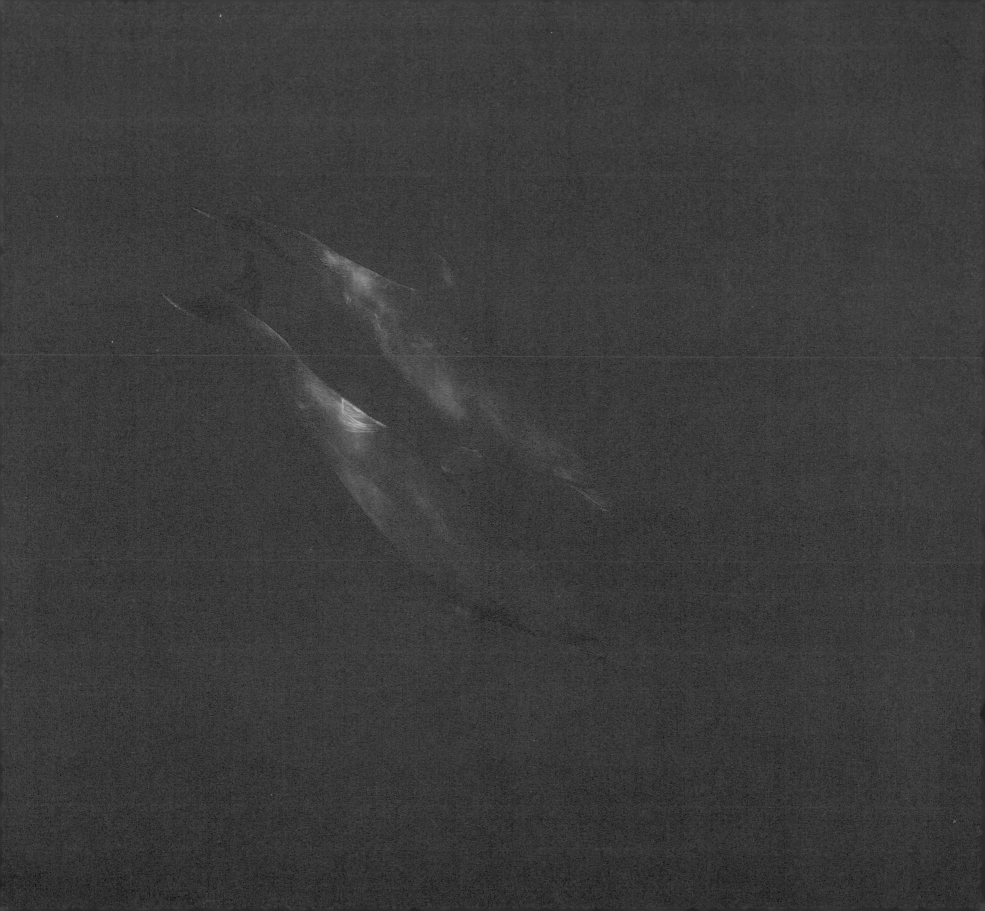

Olympic champion, no matter what stroke he or she was using and expend only one-eighth of the swimmer's energy.

The faster a dolphin swims, the more energy it spends, but very slow-moving dolphins use just about the same energy as they do when stationary. If they stop they become unstable and need to scull with flippers or make awkward tail movements just to maintain position, so in the wild they very rarely stop. Moving backwards for a dolphin is harder still, and most species cannot do it at all. This deficiency kills dolphins every day all around the world. When they blunder into submerged fishing nets and get tangled, they only have two options: to stop or keep swimming forwards. But either option results in drowning.

While dolphins have rid themselves of any need to visit the land, they are still tied to the surface of the sea, for being mammals they must breathe air. But at the same time, they are marine predators and their food lies below them in the water. To make a living, therefore, they must be expert divers too.

Diving Machines

There are several stories about a boy called Dionysios who lived in Greece in about AD 200. One day a dolphin came into the bay where he was swimming and picked him up. The dolphin swam out to sea with the terrified boy sitting on its back and then after a short trip around the bay returned him to the beach from which he had come. The boy and dolphin became friends and began regular explorations of the sea together. But were the dolphin to have dived on one of these expeditions and the boy to have kept his grip on its back, what would have happened? Common sense would tell you that the boy would have fared considerably worse than the dolphin. But why should this be? Both are mammals and judging by the species of dolphin around the Greek coast today (common or bottlenose), our two travelers would have been of similar size. So what would have happened?

Let's imagine that boy and dolphin each took a deep breath together just before they headed for the depths. To take this deep breath, both would first exhale and then inhale. In normal breathing, the boy would exchange about 5-15% of his lung volume, but because he knows that this is going to be an extra long dive he takes an extra big breath and exchanges 80%. Surprisingly, dolphins don't have overly big lungs and so our dolphin's lungs are probably similar in size to the boy's. But taking one of its normal breaths, the dolphin swaps 80-90% of the old air for new. To dive, it arches its back and lifts its tail-flukes clear of the water. The boy holds on and so down they plunge at 6 ft 6 in (2 m) a second. The insulating air in the boy's clothes quickly bubbles away and he starts to chill. The dolphin's blubber layer doesn't change at all.

With depth, the water pressure around them increases. Before they even reach 16 ft (5 m), the boy experiences an intense pain in his forehead and ears, for the air in his facial sinuses and middle ears is being compressed by the outside pressure. He has to clench his nose shut, and blow into it to force new air into the air spaces to relieve the pressure difference. The pain disappears until he gets deeper and then has to repeat his task. The dolphin, on the other hand, has well-ventilated and foam-filled facial sinuses and middle ears and so suffers no discomfort. The pressure continues to increase. Five seconds after leaving, the surface is 33 ft (10 m) above them and the pressure has doubled. It doubles again in the next 66 ft (20 m). Although the boy is doing little but hanging on, all the tissues in his body are consuming oxygen and the reserves in his lungs diminish fast. The dolphin in contrast has automatically shut down many of its organs, decreased its heart rate and just keeps the important tissues, the heart and brain irrigated; its need for oxygen fell the moment it left the surface. But on this occasion it is swimming for the two of them and so must beat its tail extra hard. Overall it uses the same oxygen as its relaxed passenger and the stores in its lungs will be getting low too. Down they continue to race.

Fifty seconds after leaving the surface they reach 330 ft (100 m) depth and the pressure around both explorers will have compressed their original gasps of air down to an eleventh of their former size and so their lungs will have collapsed. A combination of flexible ribs and strengthened lung tissue saves the dolphin from any damage. The boy's ribs and lung tissue start to bruise, but he still holds on. The oxygen stores in his lungs have almost been exhausted and his blood has built up high concentrations of carbon dioxide, giving him an intense urge to breathe. Only the remnants of oxygen in his lungs, blood and muscles keep him alive. The dolphin has a larger blood volume, a greater volume of red blood cells and muscles packed with myoglobin. As a result, both its blood and muscle each store the same quantity of oxygen as was originally kept in its lungs. The dolphin need only now tap into these reserves.

It is dark at this depth and the boy sees nothing. The dolphin has switched to its echolocation system and clicks away to itself. It has detected a school of fish to one side and a rocky pinnacle to the other.

They level out at 360 ft (110 m), less than a minute after leaving the surface. Both boy and dolphin are quite different compared to when they set out. Both have chests squeezed in by the pressure around them. The boy is pale and dizzy, the dolphin is hunting. In a moment it catches a passing fish, swallows it whole and begins the ascent to the surface. Straight away, many of the changes are reversed. The lungs of both boy and dolphin re-inflate as the air in them expands under the relaxing pressure. The light returns and the boy can see again. The air in his sinuses and middle ears will also be expanding and unless he relieves the pressure by swallowing he is liable to

burst his ear drums. He swallows, his ears pop, the pain is gone. He begins to perk up and strengthens his grip on the dolphin, but just this one exertion on top of his low oxygen reserves is too much and he blacks out, unconscious. The dolphin grips his legs with its flippers and swims on. It is now entirely using its blood and muscle oxygen stores and experiences no problems. As the couple return to the surface, two minutes after leaving it, the dolphin lets its passenger go. The light and air break his stupor. He takes a huge breath, replacing 80% of his lung volume. The dolphin takes a normal breath and does the same. The boy takes another and another but the dolphin, now free, dives immediately for ten seconds before breathing again. After a minute the boy has taken a hundred breaths and just begun to recover, but is bruised, cold and his ears are ringing. The dolphin has taken six breaths and is fully ready for another dive.

Whilst Dionysios' plunge was a very deep one for any human it is not the deepest ever. In 1996, Francisco 'Pipin' Ferreras took a two-and-a-half minute marine sled ride to 463 ft (133 m) and back on a single breath of air. But without help the deepest any breath-holding human has returned alive from has been 240 ft (73 m). For our unaided dolphin, this dive would be a warm-up. Dolphins have been tracked down to over 1795 ft (547 m) – more than half a mile (1 km) there and back – and remained submerged for over seven minutes. Just imagine it. You are at the top of the Empire State building. Your lunch is on the ground floor, 1283 ft (391 m) below. You have to charge all the way down the stairs, grab it and climb back up again on a single breath of air. Our fictitious Dionysios was lucky their trip was only to 360 ft (110 m). Incidentally, in the original story the adventure was the other way around: the dolphin followed the boy on to the beach but got itself stuck. Such are the compromises of being expert in one environment or the other.

Whilst dolphins dive to considerable depths in search of food, they must regularly return to the surface to breathe air.

Dolphins take their breaths during momentary brushes with the atmosphere which get more dramatic the faster they swim or the bigger the waves become. High-speed species, like these common dolphins, often launch themselves into the air to get a breath free from their own spray.

But no matter how excellent the dolphins have become at diving, it is easy to imagine how disadvantaged they are, compared to species which need not return to the surface to breathe. Swordfish, tuna and many sharks are of similar size to dolphins and feed on the same prey. Whilst dolphins must yo-yo between surface and depth, these fish can live alongside their quarry and need never break off a chase for air. How then do the dolphins hold their own amongst these submarine rivals? Here lies one more of the dolphins' secret weapons, and yet another legacy from their past. All mammals are warm-blooded, that is to say they keep their core body temperature almost constant, usually above ambient and for dolphins around 98°F (36-37°C). With this steady warm temperature they gain a metabolic advantage; cells and organs can be fine-tuned and efficient; complicated organs like the brain can be maintained and perhaps most importantly, muscles can work rapidly for sustained periods. Thus a warm-bodied animal can easily over-take one whose body is cold like the surrounding water. So amongst their competitors and quarry, warm-blooded dolphins have a distinct advantage. Interestingly, of all the fish only a few have evolved to have body temperatures a little higher than their surrounding water. No prizes for guessing that they are the swordfishes, tuna and sharks! But because they get their oxygen from the water through gills, built like car radiators, much of their heat is lost. Dolphins, on the other hand, can stay warm because they have no gills but take gulps of oxygen-rich air.

A Breath of Fresh Air

When at the surface, dolphins don't breathe through their mouths but through their nostrils, or to be correct, a single nostril called the blowhole. It is no longer on the end of the muzzle but exits at the top of the head roughly midway between the eyes. Normally, the blowhole is tightly shut by a plug, like a trap door, that leaves only a half-moon-shaped depression in the top of the head. When the animal breathes the plug is pulled away to reveal a circular passage that leads to the lungs. The breaths of dolphins are explosive. When they surface they exhale just before reaching the air and so the exhaled breath bursts through the water a fraction of a second before they do. With the exhaled air come thousands of tiny droplets which are shot upward like missiles. Their origin is uncertain; they may be rem-nants of water that has trickled into the blowhole during the last dive, or be mucus from the lungs, or simply be from the water that sat above the depression of the closed blowhole. Whatever their source, together with the mist from the breath, they form a visible signpost for whalers and dolphin-watchers alike.

The blows of the cetaceans vary considerably and are generally related to the size of the animal making them. Those of the great whales are huge. These geysers shoot up from the waves 26 ft (8 m) or more, leaving a mist that hangs in the air well after the whale has dived once more. The sound of a whale blowing is unforgettable, like the detonation of a distant slow-motion bomb. A dolphin's blow is a less grand affair, but remarkable just the same. The whole thing – surface, exhale, inhale and dive – is over in a fraction of a second and sounds like a steam train's chuff, suck and splosh. Afterwards, all that remains are the droplets raining back towards the sea. Sometimes individual dolphins can be told apart by the sound of their blows. Cetaceans suffer terribly from lung parasites. Most of these are nematodes, worm-like animals, which clog their airways like cooked spaghetti. When dolphins with the most heavy infestations surface, they make an asthmatic whistling noise.

In calm seas, dolphins surface with their body arched like a bridge. The beak is pushed through the water surface and they exhale as the body rolls forwards. When the head begins to point back down, they inhale and the tail nears the surface. This tumbling brush with the atmosphere is silky smooth and leaves barely a ripple. As the seas get choppy, a relaxed breath would result in lungs full of water so dolphins are more energetic and push half their bodies above the surface. In windy weather or in the open ocean, big swells develop and dolphins often surf inside them, breathing through the inclined surface, or swim against them and break through at the very crest of the wave for a breath. In this type of sea, the air is peppered with spray and inhaling it would be damaging. It is here that the bullet-like droplets in the exhalant air may have a function. As they are shot away from the blowhole they collide with the sea spray, clearing the air about to be inhaled. Neat! In storms, waves resemble charging ranks of terraced houses and the air is full of spray. Here dolphins are dwarfed, and lifting the whole back out of the water, or using 'liquid bullets', would be hopeless. Instead they burst out of the walls of water and take mid-air gasps before piling into the next wave. Seeing dolphins in a wild sea like this, is seeing them at their finest. But a mountainous sea is a terrifying place and it is only the most crazed photographers that stand on deck and risk being washed to oblivion for such pictures.

Dolphin Senses

Most dolphins are equipped with excellent sight which allows them to see well both above and below the water. Close up, their eyes look like those of a horse, large, brown and with thick eyelids. Each eye sits at the widest point of the head and can be protruded a little by swelling the tissues behind the eyeball. Many species have a visual field that stretches from ahead, all the way round 180 degrees to behind and almost straight up and straight down. This all-round view is ideal for following associates in a three-dimensional school or for spotting lurking predators. Such vision would be the envy of any school teacher. But it also has a price. With eyes covering different sides of the body, there is little capacity for binocular vision and so gauging the distance and size of an object is troublesome. Dolphins may

have got round this problem with an intriguing adaptation: a lobe of the iris in each eye can be lowered down into the middle of the normally round pupil to leave two tiny pupils at either side. Whilst the exact function of this is uncertain, having two pupils in one eye could give the dolphin a limited binocular view. Alternatively, it might allow them to focus on both close and distant objects simultaneously, say a calf close by and a shark far off. A useful trick!

As Dionysios found out on his submarine adventure, vision becomes of less and less value with depth. Pure water filters out the sun's light, selectively extracting red then orange wavelengths before eventually stealing the rest of the spectrum. But of the world's seas, the Mediterranean is one of the most transparent and many of the other waters that dolphins occupy can be pitch dark only a few body lengths below the surface. Coastal waters can be clouded by suspended sediment from rivers or wave action on loose bottom deposits and usually clear oceanic waters can become a soup of swarming plankton when warm and cold currents collide or water wells up from deeper layers. Whilst vision, in these conditions, may be useful to dolphins for identifying objects close by, it would not allow them to charge around underwater without the threat of catastrophic collisions with rocks or predators. In these circumstances, other senses must be used. Most basic of these is touch. A dolphin's skin is tremendously sensitive, particularly around the head, dorsal fin, flukes and flippers. River dolphins use a trailed flipper to guide them across the bottom whilst groups of all species swim in close formation like stunt planes, nudging each other with flippers, flukes and dorsal fin to hold position.

Touch can also be used to detect water currents, just as we can sense gusts of wind. Dolphins frequently hitch a free ride in the bulging pressure waves in front or to the sides of ships, whales or ocean swells. But bow-riding requires precise positioning to get the desired push, just as a human surfer

*Breath taking. Dolphins breathe through a single nostril on the top of the head
midway between the eyes. Normally the blowhole is shut tight by powerful muscles and a plug.
But when the animal surfaces, like the opening of an eye, the plug is pulled down and reveals a circular
passage leading to the lungs. The dolphin exhales with an explosive burst and inhales with a gasp
before the water covers over it again. And all of this can be done in less than a second.*

needs to find the correct spot on the slope of a breaker to ride it. Dolphins bow-ride ships day or night and so do not necessarily orientate by sight. Perhaps they use the feel of the swirling water around them to achieve this dare-devil feat. The skin can sense heat too, and dolphins may use thermoclines (where water masses of different temperature meet) to guide them to key feeding spots. The bristles on the beaks of young dolphins are also concerned with touch and are thought to help them feel their mother's side. In river dolphins these same bristles are maintained into adulthood and may be used to feel for prey on the bottom.

It is not at all clear whether dolphins have a sense of smell. Other vertebrates have receptors in their nostrils but because the dolphins' nostrils are now modified into the blowhole, smell could only tell them about the air above them and not the sea in which they live. Furthermore, investigations on dead animals have had little success in finding the required nerves or receptors. Dolphins do, however, have the ability to taste. They have receptors at the base of the tongue and the region of the brain associated with taste is well developed. It appears, though, that they don't have the same taste sensations that we do. Captive dolphins have demonstrated that they can taste sour things like citric acid but that they don't find it distasteful. Just imagine, if the Inuit of Greenland have over twenty names for the texture of snow, perhaps dolphins have as many sensations for the taste of a good fish!

But of all their senses, by far the most sophisticated is their hearing. Coupled with an ability to make an astonishing array of calls, dolphins, like bats, have become masters of the acoustic world. The most basic aspect of their hearing is their ability to make use of noises already in the environment. The hiss of sand swept along the sea bed may indicate where currents are strongest, whilst the roaring of swells or fizzing of rain up above can tell an animal what tactic to use when it next surfaces. Their

prey make noises too. Many bottom-living fish make grunting calls and screaming seagulls may mark fish at the surface. But more complex is the dolphins' ability to make and receive noises of their own.

If you are in a drifting boat near a school of dolphins and drop a hydrophone (underwater microphone) into the water you will be hit by a barrage of noise. Dolphins click, bark, yelp, bray, pop, whistle, mew and squeal, as if torturing a variety of farmyard animals. The high-pitched whistles of a school of spinners produces a scribbling noise like a hundred children tuning their pocket radios in and out of long-wave stations. The buzzing sounds of Risso's dolphins are like bees making short hops between flowers. Furthermore, the dolphin cacophony extends way above our own hearing range into ultra-sonic frequencies.

Despite considerable study, the functions of most of these calls are still unknown but the basics of the main types are beginning to be understood. By far the most famous are the echolocation calls that allow them to detect and follow objects in the water in front of them. They do this by making extremely loud clicking noises and then interpreting the echoes that return. We ourselves use this technique in the sonar or fish-finder systems on boats, and also in everyday life without thinking about it. If you walk into a strange, dark room, you can often tell a little about it by the echoing noise of your footsteps whilst fumbling for the light switch; the echoes in a small room sound very different to those in a large gymnasium. Dolphins have pushed this ability to extraordinary levels such that their powers of discrimination below water rival those of our eye-sight above. Early experiments showed that dolphins could maneuver around tanks whilst blindfolded without bumping into the sides or into strings hung in the water. They could also discriminate between metal spheres that to us appear almost identical in size. Furthermore, because sound travels through objects far more readily than light, they could tell whether an

object was solid or hollow. We now know that the dolphins' echolocation clicks vary depending on the species that makes them. Bottlenose dolphins produce clicks that span a wide range of frequencies, of which we can hear only the very lowest fractions, whilst Commerson's dolphins produce clicks in a narrow range of frequencies which are all far above human hearing. The reason why different species produce such different clicks is still a mystery but, interestingly, the clicks of Commerson's dolphins are almost identical to those made by harbor porpoises. Both species live in coastal areas and have bodies of similar size but they are not closely related and occupy opposite hemispheres of the earth. It has been suggested that their clicks are so similar because these sounds are best for finding food near the bottom or where there is a clutter of other noises, but another suggestion is also plausible. Being small, both Commerson's dolphins and harbor porpoises are very vulnerable to attack from killer whales. Obviously, swimming around advertizing your presence with very loud calls would be a bad idea if your predators can hear you too: like banging pots and pans together in a den of sleeping lions. Perhaps we should not be surprised to learn then that these high-frequency clicks fall just above the hearing range of killer whales.

Being able to listen to an echolocating dolphin with sophisticated equipment or just a simple microphone made waterproof with a plastic bag can tell you much about the submerged animal's behavior. A searching dolphin will produce a regular series of clicks, sounding much like a slowly revolving bicycle wheel. This is because the sound waves of each click produced must travel out to hit an object and the echoes return before the dolphin can click again. Once they have detected an object and start to approach it, they can click more rapidly, as the sound takes less and less time to go to and fro. Such approaches

sound like a door creaking and often culminate in buzzes and whines when the target is actually reached. For hunting dolphins, the number of these creaks and buzzes can give us a good indication of how often they are coming across their prey.

The mechanism by which dolphins produce their clicks has been a subject of much debate because the frequencies they produce and the rapidity of clicks have proved difficult to explain. It is clear though that the sounds are produced deep in the head, just in front of the skull and now thought to be created by an organ called the 'monkey lips' underneath the blowhole. The dish-shaped skull reflects these sounds forward to then be focused into a narrow sound beam in front of the animal by an organ called the melon. This is made up of a complex arrangement of fats and oils and acts as a sound lens, giving the dolphins their bulbous foreheads.

Unlike land mammals, dolphins don't have external ears. Instead it appears that they receive sounds with their lower jaws. Two theories currently exist on how this mechanism works. In one, sounds are picked up by the jaw bones and transmitted through the centre of each, via an oil-filled passage, to the internal ear which sits just below the eye. In the other, sound waves make the neatly spaced teeth in each lower jaw vibrate and sensory nerves then pick up their movements.

Most of the other dolphin calls (the barks, the yelps and so on) are actually made of hundreds of rapid clicks like those used in echolocation. However, there is one group of calls, the whistles, that is entirely different. Not all species are known to make them, but in those that do, they appear be a major carrier of social information. Sounding much like a high-pitched version of the whistle someone might use to summon their dog, or an attempt to tune a radio into the correct station, dolphin whistles can be made at the same time as echolocation clicks

Sleepers. It is not clear if and when dolphins sleep in the wild but now and again they can be found lying quietly at the surface.

are produced. From work on bottlenose dolphins it seems that individual dolphins adopt their own particular whistle rather like a name. These 'signature whistles' may transmit the identity of members in one group to another group, or help a calf find its mother and vice versa. By mimicking each other's whistles, it also seems that dolphins can acknowledge the presence of one another. Furthermore, subtle changes in the pitch or length of whistles might serve to transmit additional information such as alarm or dominance.

In addition to the senses already outlined, dolphins have several others. Like us, their inner ears give them a sense of balance and they can feel pain. On top of these, they may have sensations unfamiliar to us. It has been suggested, for example, they may be able to sense the magnetic field of the earth and use it to navigate through featureless oceans. More precisely, disruptions in the magnetic field, like rumples in a huge bed sheet, may supply corridors for migrating animals to follow. There are two lines of evidence that have been used to support this suggestion. Both originate from live strandings where seemingly healthy single, or groups of, animals beach themselves. The first line of evidence comes from the behavior of these animals when they are returned to the water. When pointed out to sea, they often turn and swim straight back on to the beach from which they have just come. One of the plethora of explanations for this apparently suicidal behavior is that the animals are following magnetic routes and have some-how become disorientated so that they think safety lies in the same direction as the beach. The second comes from the distribution of these strandings. One study found that live strandings tended to occur where areas of low magnetic field (the proposed corridors) crossed at right-angles to the land, whilst in areas where they ran along the coast, fewer strandings occurred. Identical studies in different parts of the world have agreed with this and others have however failed to detect a similar pattern. Consequently, the magnetic sense in cetaceans remains controversial and is often side-stepped by researchers.

However, evidence is mounting for the use of a magnetic sense in fish, birds and reptiles, and a recent study has convincingly shown its use in trout and even traced the nervous pathways from a magnetic receptor in the snout to the brain. As more is found out about this sense, the once far-fetched theory of whales and dolphins using it as a navigational aid is becoming less improbable. Setting out to prove its existence in the cetaceans is another matter. One route would be to search the bodies of dead animals and look for the cells or organs responsible. But, because magnetic fields are simple forces that change slowly in time and space, detecting them would only require a few receptor cells, a meager number of nerve fibers and a tiny amount of brain tissue. What is more, these receptors could be anywhere in the body. So finding a few tens of cells in a whale or dolphin when there are literally tens of millions between the nose and tail makes the needle in the haystack metaphor seem trivial.

Studying strandings is also problematic, because of their unpredictable nature. So the existence of this sense may never be proved – or someone might be discovering it at this very moment, such is the way of science. Whichever turns out to be the case, the presence of a magnetic sense raises some fascinating questions about what impacts human activities might have on these animals. Since the first steel ships were built, we have been continuously burying them at sea, both intentionally and otherwise. In the 1990s, two hundred and fifty a year were concealed beneath the waves. As most ships are made of steel they will alter the local magnetic field around them. So what impact might these new additions to the magnetic map be having on animals using this sense? Could they be sending migrating animals off course? Or could they be welcome signposts for animals trying to navigate in a featureless ocean? Whichever is the case,

*Dolphins are equipped with a battery of sophisticated senses: acute
eyesight both above and below water, superb underwater hearing, touch, taste, balance
and perhaps pressure and geomagnetic senses as well. They use these to orientate, hunt, avoid their
own predators and to communicate with one another. And when communicating they posture,
send complex calls (which may or may not constitute a true language), may release
pheromones, stroke, punch and often scuff each other with their teeth.*

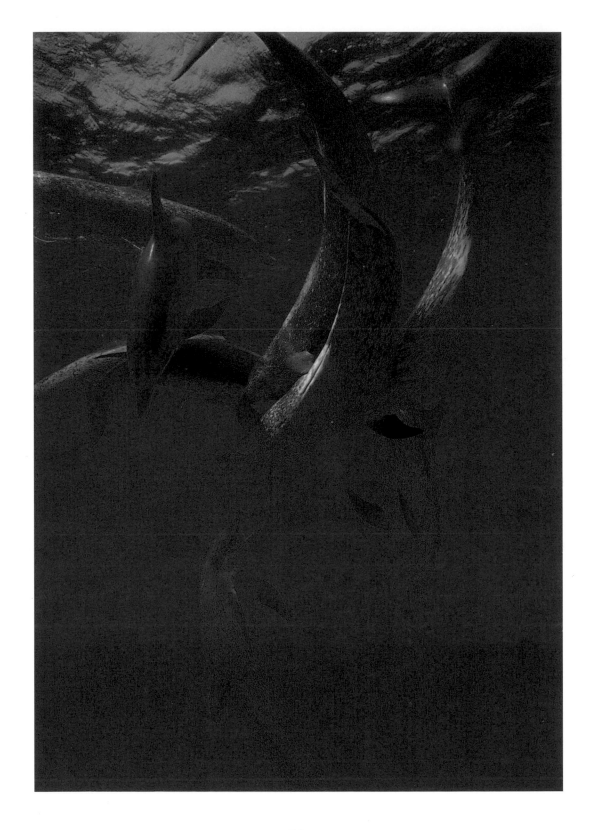

the message for us is simple: even though we do not use this sense ourselves we must not assume that other animals are oblivious to it also.

One way that is used to rank the importance of the different senses of an animal has been to measure the relative number of nerve cells dedicated to sending that information to the brain. For humans, the optic nerve (eye to brain) is the largest whereas the olfactory nerve (nose to brain) is the smallest of those known. In dolphins the order is different, the auditory nerve (ear to brain) is the largest, while the optic nerve is smaller. When sighted people think of a place or object they tend to form a visual model in their heads. Think of the inside of a car; you immediately conjure up a picture of the seats, steering wheel, wind shield and so on, then maybe later add the feel of the seats, the smell of the plastic, sound of the engine. As animals, we concentrate on our sight first, and then pay attention to our other senses later. Dolphins' biggest sensory fibers come from their ears. So perhaps they build a sound world in their heads, upon which information from the other senses is superimposed. Imagining a mental world like this adds an entirely different perspective to understanding a dolphin's life. Day is no longer very different from night, noisy environments become foggy ones, and the bodies of associates, predators and prey become transparent bundles of flesh and bones with painted wrappers.

Dolphin Intelligence

When Captain Kirk of the *Starship Enterprise* meets an intelligent alien from another planet, nine out of ten times the creature stands on legs, has a distinct head, a face, two eyes, nose (optional) and a mouth which it talks out of. Ten out of ten times the alien says something coherent. Why do we imagine intelligent life like this? Here on earth the contenders for the most intelligent life forms, that are not primates (apes, monkeys or man), have few of these traits. Dolphins don't stand on legs, usually look at you side on with just one eye, have a head that is continuous with the body, don't open their mouths to communicate and in any case, make most of their noises far outside our hearing range. Science fiction script writers, one out of ten for imagination! If Kirk had come back to earth and met a dolphin, would he, his team, or the onboard computer have been able to decipher anything meaningful from what it might have said? This question lurks, like a Klingon ship, at the sidelines of dolphin research and is large in the popular imagination.

In ancient times, the intelligence and emotional capabilities of animals were assumed. Pliny explained the death of a dolphin, following the demise of a human associate, as a suicide out of 'sorrow and regret'. Since then we have found that most of the animal kingdom behave in a more mechanical manner without reasoning or emotional intent. With this recognition, the hunt for an intellectual companion to ourselves began. It makes intuitive sense that brain size is linked with intelligence, but it is also clear that brain size is linked with body size. Big dogs aren't necessarily any smarter than small dogs. It is the animals with big brains in relation to their bodies that are the likely master-minds and the primates and cetaceans have the biggest brain to body ratios of all. The human brain weighs in at 1.9% of our body weight, whilst a bottlenose dolphin attains a score of 0.95%. A horse on the other hand only measures 0.15%. But within the cetaceans, there is a wide variety of values. For example, the baleen whales may have big brains but they also have huge bodies and score as little as 0.007%. Incidentally, Captain Kirk in one film did meet a baleen whale (a humpback) but having a brain weight to body ratio of 0.02% it was a poor contender for

Complex social interactions typify dolphin societies: an animal may be ostracized by a group and then welcomed back.

meaningful conversation. Generally, the toothed whales attain higher scores, often greater than those of primates and this is where the problems really begin. How can we compare a dolphin's brain with a chimp's? Their sizes may be similar but their construction is not. Dolphin brains carry many primitive features whilst others are more complex; for example, they have fewer neurones for a given volume of brain tissue but each may transmit impulses faster. Comparing anatomy cannot provide all the answers; instead, we could look at their behavior for clues.

Dolphins are renowned for being curious, can mimic, have good memories and can distinguish between members of their species as well as human swimmers, boats and so on. But all of these traits are common in the animal kingdom; parrots show similar aptitudes. Dolphins do occasionally use tools, but their use is not particularly complex either. So what do dolphins do with their big brains? One possibility is that living in a three-dimensional environment requires superior computing power, but fish don't have large brains. Nor does the use of echolocation, as bats and their small brains demonstrate. The complexity of dolphins' other vocalizations has led to suggestions that they might have some form of language, but all attempts to prove this have failed. Dolphins in captivity have shown that they can understand simple sentences and syntax, as in the difference between 'take the surfboard to the ball' and 'take the ball to the surfboard'. And furthermore, when asked to perform a leap or turn of their own choice, they can somehow communicate it to a companion and perform it in synchrony without practice. But claims that dolphins might exchange secrets about the meaning of life are no longer proposed by anyone but the fanciful.

One area of dolphin life that appears to be more complex than that of most other animals and which rivals that of primates, is their social lives. The more we find out about dolphin social interactions, the more we discover how complex they are. In oceanic and coastal species, each dolphin may have several hundred associates and with each it may have a different relationship. It is distinctly possible that big brains are needed to manage this information. Furthermore, the interactions between individuals appear to be highly dependent on the context within which the animals find themselves, as work on wild bottlenose dolphins off western Australia is beginning to demonstrate. There, male dolphins form alliances of pairs or trios within which the partners act like buddies looking out for one another. These small teams may be effective at controlling the movements of females with whom they intend to mate and also for excluding other males with similar intentions. In the breeding season, competition for access to female dolphins is extremely intense and it is at this time that some of the most remarkable interactions have been observed. In one, two males came across another alliance escorting a female. The two males could not capture the female from the alliance in possession so they co-opted the help of a third alliance to make themselves into a team of four and successfully attacked the alliance with the female. Outnumbered, the males that were originally in possession were forced to leave. The team of four then split up and our original pair took possession of the female. Such behavior suggests that dolphins have some powers of reasoning, can foresee the outcome of their actions, can communicate intentions to each other and can perhaps store up favors!

Whilst their social lives may explain the large brains of dolphins, the question of how intelligent they are has still not been answered. This is because it is probably impossible to solve. The brains of different animals have evolved to do different things. How would we fare if given the blindfolded assignment of remembering the echoes of a range of steel balls and then figuring out which one would best fit into a hole? I'm sure that even Captain Kirk or the wondrous Mr Spock would fare badly!

From Birth to Death

If you come across a school of fish in the open sea, the chances are that each individual will look like any other, for fish in schools are often all of the same generation. A single school of dolphins, on the other hand, is likely to contain a jumble of adults, juveniles and calves. And furthermore, some will be relatives — brothers, sisters or mothers — and others total genetic strangers. The closest bond in these multi-layered societies is that between mothers and their calves; all other aspects of dolphin society are built around this basic foundation block.

Being aquatic mammals, females cannot build nests or burrows in which to calve but must give birth and raise their young in the open water. The calves also must be able to swim, breathe, suckle, see, feel and hear straight away and so are born fully formed and ready for action. A litter of small calves could not keep up with the mother's school and would quickly lose their heat to the water, so females put all their efforts into producing just one large calf at a time. Twins are occasionally born but rarely survive. Furthermore, with bigger calves being better than small ones there is a strong pressure for females to produce as large a calf as possible and so they produce ones that are big even in comparison to themselves. Commerson's dolphins, for example, produce calves about half as long as they are themselves. Large calves need long gestation periods which are usually between ten and fourteen months. In contrast, the birth itself is quick. Without a constricting pelvis, labor and birth may be over in less than an hour and it is little wonder that this facet of dolphin life is rarely seen in the wild. Calves are born more commonly tail rather than head first and, despite their fins and flukes being crumpled from the confines of the womb, they must swim the moment they hit the water. Like the wings of a butterfly emerging from a chrysalis, the dorsal fin and flukes are quickly pumped up by blood pressure, for when the umbilical cord breaks, the calf no longer has a supply of oxygen and must reach the surface under its own propulsion to fill its lungs with air for the first time.

In the week following birth, mother and calf are inseparable. The calf swims beside her just behind the dorsal fin and a little above or below her mid-line. In this position, their color and outline blend, camouflaging the calf from predators. It can also ride in her slipstream and be transported, literally, without moving a muscle. When she breathes, the calf breathes at the corresponding point on her roll. Breathing is most difficult for newborns because their small size makes getting the head clear of the water troublesome, so very young animals burst out and breathe before their chins slap back into the water. But mother and offspring cannot stay continually pinned to one another. Young calves are feeble divers and so every dive or two they must break away and take an extra breath. The calf also has to interrupt its ride when it suckles, for the female's mammary glands exit through slits either side of the genital opening underneath her. Suckling takes place either stationary or on the move. Milk is squirted directly into the calf's mouth and young dolphins' tongues have a frilled margin to make a seal. Dolphin milk, like that of other marine mammals, is extremely rich and contains up to ten times the fat and protein of the milk in land mammals. Although each suckling bout lasts for only a few seconds, a calf is entirely dependent on this milk for at least a year or longer after birth. This places a fearsome drain on the energy reserves of the mother, who must, after all, maintain herself as well. She must soon resume foraging, but this poses a problem. If she is to be effective she must leave her calf at the surface and so expose it to danger. The extent of this threat varies considerably with the habitat that the dolphin uses. For river dolphins, their freshwater homes are generally shallow and predators rare and so leaving a calf for a moment or two poses few risks. In the open sea, where sharks and killer whales are an ever-present threat and food may be far below, leaving a calf alone long enough to feed would soon end in disaster. But in these situations all female dolphins face the same dilemma, so they form cooperative groups and each intersperses guarding with bouts of foraging. An adult female may also co-opt her previous offspring to do the same, which for the offspring is not as altruistic as it might appear, for it is in their genetic interests to help a brother or sister. Other female dolphins are also able to offer more than just their attention and when exposed to orphaned calves can spontaneously produce milk. Similarly, elderly adult female pilot whales (themselves close relatives to most dolphins) retain their ability to produce milk long after they have lost the capacity to produce calves of their own.

Certainly helping others would make a lot of sense, particularly if the baby-sitters and milk donors were relatives, or if it earns return favors, but little in animal behavior is quite as simple as it first appears. Recent studies of bottlenose dolphins in Australia have shown that some apparent baby-sitting is actually kidnapping and ends with chases and attacks from the mother. Inexperienced females, it seems, may practice parenting with another dolphin's calf, rather than learning on their own off-spring. Despite these liberties, the benefits of female cooperation are clear and studies in Florida have shown that bottlenose dolphins born into tight-knit female groups have a higher chance of survival than those that are not. Thus the benefits of cooperative rearing bind females together and so a shell of associations is formed around the mother-calf bonds.

Adult males, whilst associating with groups of females or moving between them, appear to have no active role in repro-duction after mating. Indeed, studies on bottlenose dolphins in Florida have shown that the fathers of calves tend to come from and return to completely different areas. Furthermore, because a female may mate with many males, no male can be sure whether he is the father of any particular calf or not. This promiscuous activity has traditionally been thought to ensure that a female maximizes the chance of becoming pregnant during the narrow windows of opportunity given by her reproductive cycle. But we now realize that it may also serve to confuse males so that they cannot know whether or not they are the father of any particular calf. For whilst this excludes any incentive for a male to invest energy in looking after a calf, it also reduces the chances of infanticide. There is a strong genetic payoff for a male that comes across a female with young, to kill the offspring. Robbed of her calf, that female must then quickly become fertile again if she is to pass on her own genes. The killing male now has a chance to be the father. This pattern of male infanticide is most famous in lion prides where males that have just evicted a previous male kill all of his cubs and then mate with the lionesses. Since its recognition, this phenomenon has been found all over the animal kingdom from sparrows to bears. Given that dolphins are ultimately governed by their need to pass on their own genes, there is no reason to believe that they should be any different. Indeed recent evidence from dolphins off Scotland suggests that infanticide is a feature of dolphin societies and provides another reason for females to form groups to defend their offspring from males intent on fatherhood. Dolphin societies are clearly not the utopian civilizations that many daydreamers would have us believe!

Mating, when it occurs, is belly to belly and takes place on the move. Intromission may last anything from seconds to minutes but is often broken by the need of one or other partner to breathe. There appear to be varying amounts of courtship before mating, with males making elaborate swimming patterns and calls. Whether these are to impress a female of a male's

Hanging on to its mother's coat tails: like most other species, young dusky dolphins take several years to reach sufficient maturity to fend for themselves. In the intervening time they stay with their mother and become part of her social circle.

fitness or a signal to other dolphins that that male has coupled with that female is unknown. Trying to understand what is going on in these relationships is difficult. Studies of captive dolphins have given many clues as to the types of behavior we should expect to see, but in most situations only a few dolphins are present, all usually have prior knowledge of one another and none have an opportunity to leave should they wish to. Any signals between these animals could therefore be subtle or, by the same token, be highly exaggerated. To confuse matters further, copulation in dolphin societies occurs more frequently than it would if it had a purely procreative role. Females have a short period in every few years in which they are fertile but they mate often in the intervening periods; furthermore mating also happens between brothers and sisters, mothers and calves and same sex couples. It appears, therefore, that mating probably has a more social role in dolphin societies than it does in our own and is perhaps more akin to the mutual grooming seen among the apes, horses, cats and other mammals. Distinguishing between procreative and social mating requires some other information on the female's reproductive condition. The most precise could be obtained by measuring hormone levels in her blood or urine. Again there are such opportunities in captive dolphins but the logistics of measuring them in wild animals in the open sea are mind boggling. A more practical solution is to record the behaviors between males and females and then catch up with the female later to see if she is accompanied by a calf. Subtracting the gestation period from the date of the birth will indicate when she was fertile and hence what state she was in when the original observations were made. Understandably this process is slow and painstaking and explains why we know so little about how dolphins choose their mates.

Although calves are born fully formed, they are noticeably different from adults. Overall their bodies tend to be more chubby and their heads are bigger relative to the rest of the body. The dorsal fin, if present, is more triangular and the body color differs. Spotted dolphins, for example, are born without spots and gradually gain them until, as adults, they resemble a snowstorm. Likewise, Risso's dolphins are born a very plain gray but any skin damage produces brilliant white scars. Adults end up almost pure white after a lifetime of being bitten by one another. Calves of all species are born with a series of five to eight light vertical bands called fetal folds that run up and down either flank. Thought to be from the skin creases that occur in the mother's womb, they clearly distinguish a calf from other dolphins for its first three to eighteen months of life.

Weaning is a slow process, with a solid diet gradually replacing its mother's milk over a period of months or years. All of this time, the young dolphin remains under its mother's care and may stay with her for several further years while it acquires the social and physical skills essential later on. A female may become pregnant again or even be suckling a new calf before the last leaves to join other juveniles. But despite this overlap, breeding is a slow and energetically expensive process as she can only produce a single calf every one-and-a-half to four years. Larger species produce as few as seven calves in a lifetime. For the now-independent juvenile, growing up must happen as fast as possible if it is not to succumb to starvation and predation. It will reach physical maturity between the ages of five and thirteen years but full breeding maturity can take much longer, possibly even 20 years for male bottlenose dolphins.

Because females are only receptive for short periods in their breeding cycle, available female mates are effectively rare in comparison to the number of males ready to reproduce. Considerable competition may develop between males and in

A young bottlenose dolphin hitches a free ride in its mother's slipstream.

most mammals culminates in physical contests which favor huge and powerful males. A single male elephant seal, for example, can weigh more than three females put together. In dolphins, these pressures are present too, but for a variety of reasons are apparently less intense. In the bigger species, like the bottlenose and Risso's dolphins, males are subtly larger than females and are the most heavily scarred. In the smallest species, like the Commerson's, Hector's and river dolphins, quite different factors must be at work because males can be as much as 15% smaller than females. Why this is the case, however, is not fully under- stood. Perhaps in these species it is the males that are actually the optimal size for general living and it is females that are forced to be larger by the need to reproduce. The small calf produced by a small female may be just too inadequate to survive.

Being slow to grow and reproduce, dolphins accordingly must have long lifespans. But finding out exactly what these are is not straightforward. One way is to follow an individual until it dies, but having longevities perhaps similar to our own, few research studies (or careers for that matter) continue long enough. A simpler way is to decode the information stored in their teeth. Toothed cetaceans are born with a set that they retain for life. When first formed the teeth are hollow with an enamel shell and an inner lining of dentine. As the animal grows older, it lays down regular layers of dentine on the inside of each tooth. Cutting a tooth from top to bottom reveals these layers and counting them will give the age. Simple! Getting hold of teeth is not difficult either because stranded or captured animals are common. But working out how often the layers are deposited is more complicated. One way is to use tetracycline. When children are given a course of this antibiotic, minute quantities are deposited in their teeth, leaving bands which glow under ultraviolet light. If a dolphin is captured and given an antibiotic shot, it too will incorporate the dye along with the latest tooth layer. When it eventually dies and is recovered, the

number of layers after the dyed one gives the deposition rate. In bottlenose dolphins one layer is put down a year, in others it is every two, while in many it is still unknown. For the species in which the rates are established, the oldest known dolphin in the wild (an adult female) was calculated to have lived for 51 years. For most individual dolphins, however, life is far shorter.

The two most dangerous periods in a dolphin's life occur when it is newborn and when it has just become independent from its mother. For these age groups, attack from sharks, killer whales and perhaps members of their own species are an ever- present threat. Starvation is also a continuous danger. If a calf is separated from its mother any time before it is properly weaned, it will probably starve. Similarly, when food supplies become limited it is often the least experienced animals that suffer most. Once dolphins have survived these hurdles, death may be less imminent, but there is still a catalog of dangers awaiting them and each year those posed by humans become ever more prominent on this list.

Like all wild animals, the bodies of dolphins provide a temp- orary or permanent home to a myriad of other organisms. Remora fish stick on to their skin to hitch a free ride and some protection. Other fish, like lampreys and cookie-cutter sharks, also attach themselves but take a bite of flesh away with them, leaving the circular wounds visible on many dolphins. Although these injuries are small, an unprotected opening represents a doorway through which fungal, bacterial and viral diseases can invade. As a consequence dolphins have evolved tremendous powers of regeneration. When human skin is damaged, clotted blood and proteins form a scab under which the skin is regenerated. In water, these scabs turn soggy and wash away. As many sailors have found out, minor wounds can quickly become debilitating sores. In dol- phins, skin damage elicits a different response; the cells surrounding the wound immediately die and form a protective and inert shield that doesn't wash away.

*In the early 1990s hundreds of dead and dying striped dolphins
washed ashore around the Mediterranean coasts of Spain, France and Italy. Although
the dolphins were dying of a viral infection, other parasites, starvation and man-made
pollutants may have weakened them and so contributed to the outbreak.*

An example of regeneration following a devastating injury occurred to a bottlenose dolphin which lived off the east coast of England. This animal, named 'Freddie', lived in a harbor mouth and regularly swam with humans and boats. It often hung in the bubbles produced by propellers but received massive injuries when the driver of one boat, unaware of the dolphin, switched from motoring ahead to astern. The dolphin was sucked between the two propellers, and received eleven cuts along its right flank; some completely penetrated the skin and blubber and entered the underlying muscle. Despite being continually exposed to water and permeated with sand, the smallest wounds had healed within a month and the larger within five months. Similar injuries to a human, kept in water, would certainly have been fatal.

Nevertheless, a huge variety of pathogens (of which only a tiny fraction have been identified) can breach dolphin defences. In them we find many diseases common to land-mammals including ourselves. Fungal infections, like Candida (which causes thrush in humans), and bacteria like Staphylococci and Streptococci that cause pneumonia and other diseases, are common in dolphins. Others appear to be specific to marine mammals, if not to individual species. The contagious bacteria which cause brucellosis and result in abortions in cattle, have been found in a wide range of marine mammals including dolphins. On close examination, though, the strains found in dolphins are subtly different from those in farm animals and probably reflect their different biology. However, as we are beginning to find out from our meat industry, there is no reason to assume that diseases cannot cross the species divide with devastating consequences. For obvious reasons, then, it is always advisable to take precautions when handling dolphins and other marine mammals, living or dead. Covering wounds, wearing gloves and keeping clear of their blows makes good sense, but it is often forgotten that live dolphins are just as likely to catch something from us as we are from them. Breathing over them and poking wounds can do little good. Furthermore, our worldwide policy of discharging raw sewage into the sea, subjects most coastal dolphins to our germs with impacts that are little known and rarely considered by governments or planners.

In addition to the microscopic, the bodies of dolphins play host to a vast array of larger parasites that include amphipods, barnacles, flat worms, hook worms, mites, nematodes and tape worms. The burdens of these parasites can be astonishing; when a 6½ ft (2 m) striped dolphin was dissected it provided enough parasites to fill two-thirds of a bucket. But despite this burden, the dolphin could swim, dive and reproduce, for such infestations are normal. It died, however, because of a viral infection of the type which caused an epidemic in the Mediterranean Sea in 1990 and 1991. Over 1100 animals washed ashore dead or dying on the coasts of Spain, France and Italy but to this day it is uncertain what exactly led to the outbreak. While it is clear that the immediate origin was a morbillivirus of a type similar to that which causes distemper in dogs, other findings suggest that the outbreak might have been more complicated and the virus simply a final straw. Many animals were severely malnourished, some very heavily parasitized and the tissues of every individual contaminated with man-made toxic pollutants. These chemicals took a variety of forms, including pesticides and industrial waste products, which are known to compromise the abilities of mammals to fight infection. So although the viral outbreak appeared to be a natural phenomenon, its devastating impact may have been heightened by human interference. In fact, human activities through over-fishing, net entanglement, noise, chemical, plastic and oil pollution, directed hunts, explosions and boat strikes have altered the life of most dolphins. While no species have yet become extinct, several are teetering on the very edge and the magnitude of these threats varies with the habitats that each species occupies.

Oceanic Dolphins

An Oceanic Dolphin's World

Imagine you are standing in a flat grassy field. Now imagine that the grass continues over the featureless horizon in every direction for thousands of miles. Above you looms an empty blue sky and there is not a breath of wind. Now imagine you are lying down in that field, looking into the blue infinity above. Next, turn the whole image upside down so that the endless field is a ceiling, to which you are pinned, and the sky now a blue void below. Imagine this and you can begin to picture the home of the oceanic dolphins: an abode so vast that individuals may go through their entire lives without ever experiencing the bottom or sides of their water-world. The oceans are the biggest habitat that the earth can offer. The Atlantic, Pacific, Indian, Arctic and Southern Oceans not only cover an area twice as large as all the land masses put together, but have an average depth of 2½ miles (4 km) and in parts can reach Everest-swallowing depths of 6 miles (10 km) and more.

Because no storms or waves can stir the distant bottom of these oceans, material that sinks into them rarely comes back to the surface. Plankton, fish, birds and cetacean droppings as well as their dead bodies, sediment from the land and dust from the air are all sucked by gravity into this enormous trap. Consequently, the surface waters are poor in the nutrients needed by planktonic algae to flourish and so the water is left clear and blue. As algae form the base of most marine food chains, the oceans are nutritional deserts and hunting is a major occupation. In a few exceptional areas, upwelling currents bring nutrients back to the surface and algae bloom. But even in these areas, the food chain works in two directions. For all oceanic animals except those at the very top, each hunter is also the hunted. Even the great white shark must watch its back for killer whales.

Oceanic waters, like our endless upside-down field and sky, present few places to hide. Waves, however, offer one refuge. In the same way as it is hard for a rescue-boat to find a dinghy in big breakers, so some animals, like the flying fish, seek shelter by keeping among the undersides of waves. But, just as rescuers will use a spotter plane to guide them to the distressed craft, a predator can dive a little deeper to look up and see their prey above them. Another option is to use the enormous depth. No matter how pure any water is, it absorbs light and even in the clearest seas, darkness prevails only a few hundred feet below the surface. Diving down into this dark water may be a good option, but there are no algae at these depths. So hiding in the dark water is like hiding in the basement at a dinner party and there is no benefit in avoiding predators if you starve in the process. Instead many animals live in the depths during the day and migrate upwards to feed during the cover of night. This migrating band of crustaceans, fish and squid is almost universal in the oceans and is called the deep scattering layer. It can easily be detected with a boat's echo-sounder. But hiding in the depths is not an option for animals that feed by sight or are tied to the surface for air. Instead they must ride out their days in full view of both their predators and their prey and despite these odds, many animals have become expert at it. Included in these are dolphins.

The Species

Of the 30 dolphin species covered in this book, around two-thirds are from time to time found in the open oceans. But only 14 have accomplished full-time life in this environment; these are the true oceanic dolphins.

Spinner dolphins occur in tropical, sub-tropical and sometimes warm temperate regions of the Atlantic, Indian and Pacific Oceans. Their habit of making exuberant leaps was first noted by a Benedictine monk in 1769 who said that they 'sprang out of the water in an extraordinary manner'. They 'leaped at least three or four feet high and turned round not less than three times in the air, as if they had been on a spit'. These characteristic leaps which involve rotating up to four times on their long axis, have led to their name. Spinners are slender with a long thin beak and have a streamlined 6 ft 6 in- (2 m-) long body, built for speed.

Despite an earth-girdling range, spinners are genetically similar to one another and so are defined as one biological species. However, their appearance varies depending on where they come from. Eastern spinners, for example, live in areas of the Pacific seaward of Central America and Mexico, and have only two small patches of white on an otherwise entirely battleship-gray body. In contrast, Hawaiian spinners have a striking three-tone color pattern with a dark back, white belly and gray sides. Whitebelly spinners, which live between Hawaii and Peru, are intermediate in color pattern. In addition, the body size and shape of different forms also varies. Whitebelly spinners are more robust than their eastern cousins, while the dwarf spinners of the Gulf of Thailand are only about two-thirds the length of the other forms.

With their enormous range it follows that spinners also live in a variety of habitats. Most live in the oceans, where they feed on small fish, squid and crustaceans living in the deep scattering layer. During the day, this layer is far below the dolphins and out of reach. But as it migrates upward at dusk to within a few hundred feet of the surface, it comes within the dolphins' diving range. At dawn the layer retreats back into the depths and the spinners spend their day in large schools, often associating with other species of dolphin until the next night's feeding can begin. Where spinners live near oceanic islands, they may retreat to

bays for their daily rests and swim in clear, shallow waters with an unobstructed sandy bottom so that approaching sharks cannot take them by surprise. In some areas, spinners also make use of coral reefs and feed on the small fish that live around them.

In the Atlantic Ocean, one form of spinner has become sufficiently different from the others to merit its designation as a species in its own right. The Clymene dolphin is named either after the daughter of Oceanus and Tethys in Greek mythology or from the Greek 'Klymenos' meaning famous or notorious. Whilst first identified in 1846 from a collection of bones, the actual existence of this dolphin was disputed until 1981 when its living appearance was first documented. Clymene dolphins look much like the Hawaiian form of the spinner dolphin but have shorter beaks. They live in the deep tropical and subtropical waters of the Atlantic Ocean from New Jersey in the north to southern Brazil in the south, Texas in the west and Senegal in the east. Very little is known about their behavior, although several groups have stranded themselves on north American coasts, and the stomach contents from one animal suggest that they may have a similar diet to most spinner dolphins.

Clymene and spinners share much of their range with pantropical spotted dolphins, but these animals look very different to the two already described. They are slightly larger – up to 8 ft (2.5 m) long – have a heavier build and their color pattern evolves as they age. Born with a gray back and pale belly, they gradually develop a snow-storm pattern of white and black spots over their entire bodies. These dolphins are highly social and congregate into schools of hundreds or even thousands of individuals. But unlike the spinner or Clymene dolphins, they tend to feed day and night on deep-water as well as surface-dwelling species including frigate tuna, squid and flying fish. Pantropical spotteds often associate with other species of dolphin and below them frequently swim adult yellowfin tuna. The relationship between dolphins and tuna must be one of

The old school ties. For oceanic species like these spinner dolphins, a school is more than just a collection of animals, it is a functional unit across which information on predators is passed, foraging is co-ordinated and the duties of parenthood shared.

*Lost in space? The methods used by dolphins to navigate across the oceans are
mysterious. The bottom of most oceans can be 2 miles (3.5 km) or more below the surface and
the sides hundreds or even thousands of miles away. Currents are predictable signposts but without
a fixed point of reference, their motion is undetectable. Consequently efforts to understand marine animal
navigation have turned to less tangible parameters; the earth's magnetic fields, the shape of waves or the
taste of the water. But whichever combination they use, it is difficult to believe that purposeful-looking
oceanic dolphins like this pantropical spotted dolphin may have no clue where they are going!*

the oceans' most well studied, but still unsolved mysteries. It is even uncertain who is following whom in the relationship and what benefit either party gains from their association is still unclear. Current thinking suggests that it is the tuna which follow the dolphins and that it is the superior searching and predator-detection abilities of the dolphins that the tuna exploit. However, having hundreds or thousands of hungry tuna following the dolphins around and competing with them for food must give the dolphins some advantages or they would surely not tolerate this trailing entourage. Perhaps the tuna act as unwitting sentinels or decoys for sharks approaching from below, perhaps the tuna make prey more available to the dolphins by driving it towards the surface, or perhaps it is that the dolphins simply cannot shake off the tuna? What is even more strange is that oceanic tuna also congregate below floating logs, rubbish or other debris. Hundreds of tons of fish can be found circling a single floating tree trunk in the open ocean. Whilst these behaviors are little understood, they have been heavily exploited by our fisheries and have led to some severe consequences for many oceanic dolphins, particularly for the pantropical spotted and eastern spinner dolphins.

In the Atlantic Ocean, pantropical spotted dolphins share their range with Atlantic spotted dolphins. As their name suggests, Atlantic spotteds are similar in appearance and size to their pantropical counterparts, but have a slightly heavier build and a pale band on their skin which extends from their flanks up towards the dorsal fin. Like the pantropical spotteds, they become progressively more speckled with age and sexual maturity and the degree to which they change varies depending on where they live. Atlantic spotteds living near the coastal margins are slightly larger, more spotty, have stouter beaks and larger teeth than the same species in the open oceans. Like the spinners, some populations use shallow areas of water to spend their days socializing and resting. But they also feed in these

shallow areas and have been watched digging their beaks, heads and even shoulders into the sand to catch burrowing animals. Their predictable use of shallow offshore sand banks for these activities has provided some unrivalled opportunities to study their behavior. In these studies, Atlantic spotted dolphins have often been observed interacting with bottlenose dolphins. This contact varies from the affiliative to the highly aggressive. The bottlenose are larger and more robust than the spotted dolphins and have stubby beaks. They have dark gray backs, lighter gray flanks, a pale belly and, in most cases, no spots.

Bottlenose dolphins not only share their range with Atlantic spotted dolphins, they have a truly global range that overlaps that of most other dolphin species, making them the all-rounders of the dolphin world. Like the spinner dolphins, they vary in size from 6 ft 6 in to 13 ft (2 to 4 m) long with their shape and color depending on where they are found. This has prompted suggestions that they may represent as many as 20 or more different species, whilst others argue that instead they represent just a single one. Conflicting results from studies of skull development and genetic makeup continue to fuel this debate. Whichever is the case, bottlenose dolphins that originate from coastal areas appear different to those of the open oceans. Oceanic bottlenose dolphins generally have darker bodies, narrower flippers, fins and flukes and are often larger than the inshore representatives. They also differ physiologically with offshore animals, having an extra type of haemoglobin in their blood which may make them better divers or more tolerant to the cold temperatures they experience when diving deep into the water.

Because of their huge range, primarily coastal habits and tolerance to life in captivity, bottlenose dolphins are without doubt the best studied of all the dolphin species. In complete contrast, hourglass dolphins are probably the least well known. These strikingly colored animals live only in the Southern

Ocean, and only in waters below about 50°F (10°C). They rarely come close to any land and so few carcasses have ever been recovered from beaches for study. They are small dolphins, up to 5 ft 6 in (1.7 m), with a big dorsal fin, and, except for their pale belly, are jet black all over with two brilliant white patches on their flanks in a characteristic hourglass pattern, giving them their name. Fraser's dolphins are similar to hourglass dolphins in that they are little known, with fewer than fifty specimens existing in museum collections. These animals appear to live in the world's very warmest waters, right at the equator. They have a gray back and black band leading from the front of the blunt head, over the eye and down the flank towards the tail. They appear to be particularly common in the western Pacific around the Philippines and Indonesia and are thought to be deep divers because the types of fish, shrimps and squid found in their stomachs usually live more than 820 ft (250 m) below the surface. Schools of Fraser's dolphins are usually large and can contain a hundred or more individuals and they frequently swim alongside other species of dolphin and whale.

Pacific white-sided dolphins, as their name suggests, live only in the Pacific and then only in its northern part from the Gulf of California to the Aleutian Islands and directly westward across the Pacific rim to Japan and Taiwan. They are stocky dolphins, about 7 ft (2 m) long, with a pattern of gray and black patches over their back and flanks. They feed on small schooling fish and squid down to depths of 650 ft (200 m) or more and swim in large energetic schools. Across their range, they are highly abundant and often associate with northern right whale dolphins which share a similar range but look entirely different. For dolphins about 8 ft (2.4 m) long, northern right whale dolphins are incredibly slender with tiny tails and no dorsal fin at all. As they course through the waves, they look more like a school of huge penguins than dolphins and to extend the similarity, have an almost identical black and white tuxedo color pattern. They

have a similar diet to oceanic spinner dolphins and, like them, are regularly seen in schools of many hundreds of individuals. Southern right whale dolphins are very much like their northern counterparts, but have a greater amount of white on their belly and sides and live only in the southernmost parts of the Pacific, Atlantic and Indian Oceans as well as the Southern Ocean itself.

Common dolphins, as their name suggests, are abundant across their enormous range. They live in the Atlantic, Indian and Pacific Oceans and most seas except those at the poles. Their distribution appears to be bounded by low water temperatures and during the summer months they often use warm currents to migrate into higher latitudes such as the North Sea off Europe, southern Norway and Newfoundland. Like the spinners, there are several races (and perhaps species) of common dolphin based on differences in their skull characteristics, number of teeth and details of pigmentation. However all appear basically similar. They are muscular but streamlined medium-sized dolphins, about 6.2 ft (1.9 m) long, with distinct beaks adorned with as many as two hundred sharp teeth, and they have a characteristic color pattern. The beak, flippers, dorsal fin and tail are jet black, the belly is white and their sides from the snout to middle are buff-colored whilst further back they are light gray. Above this is a dark cape that covers the animal's back and extends down below the dorsal fin. In doing so, it joins an extension of the white belly patch, bisecting the buff and gray side panels and giving common dolphins their distinctive crossed color pattern. Their dorsal fins are tall and some animals have a pale patch in the centre. Generally, common dolphins live in deep oceanic waters or on their margins and prefer areas where the water temperatures and productivity are more seasonally variable than spinner and spotted dolphins. Like other oceanic species, they have a diet that includes schooling small fish and squid which they catch between the surface and about 980 ft (300 m) depth.

*Fraser's dolphins are clearly distinguished from other species by a thick black stripe that separates their gray
backs from their pale bellies. Whole schools of these highly social dolphins disappear from the surface at once to feed
at depth and then reappear at the surface in a frenzy of synchronized breathing before disappearing once more.*

Common dolphins are sometimes seen in association with striped dolphins, which share similar habitat preferences although the latter do not tend to stray as far into temperate waters and seem to seek out areas where cold and warm currents collide. Where striped dolphins occur they can be very abundant and are the third or fourth most abundant species in the eastern tropical Pacific and the most in the western and central Mediterranean. Like other oceanic dolphins, striped are highly social and schools of a hundred or more are common. They feed on small fish and squid in the deep scattering layer, of which many, like the lanternfish, carry light-producing organs.

Striped dolphins have black backs, gray flanks and a white belly but superimposed on this is a black stripe that runs from the beak, through the eye to the tail. Another stripe runs from the eye a short way towards the belly and a third from the eye to the pectoral flippers. Although striped dolphins can be boisterous around boats, they can also be shy and unapproachable in areas where they have been hunted.

Risso's dolphins are quite unlike most other oceanic dolphin species. Seen against the light, they can be mistaken for killer whales as they slowly roll at the surface. But, when observed close up, they cannot be mistaken for anything but themselves. Risso's have blunt, bulbous heads and large stocky bodies with a base color of gray. Etched on this are hundreds of white scars. The pigment in their skin is not replaced after damage, and as they get older the scars build up until their bodies are almost pure white. The damage, it seems, comes from the teeth of other Risso's dolphins. This species feeds primarily on squid, and appears not to need the numerous needle-like teeth characteristic of the fish-eating dolphins. Instead, Risso's have seven or fewer blunt pairs of teeth in their lower jaws and none at all in their upper jaws. Another group of squid-eating cetaceans, the beaked whales, have taken this tooth reduction to an extreme

– only males have erupted teeth and even then they only have two which are developed into a pair of tusks. Being unnecessary for feeding, the teeth may now be used as weapons for fighting and so the scars are thought to display its age to other opponents, or how many battles a Risso's dolphin or beaked whale has had in the past.

Rough-toothed dolphins appear to be intermediates between Risso's and other oceanic dolphins. They have about ninety teeth and live on a mixed diet that includes a large fraction of squid. They also keep their scars and often behave like Risso's dolphins, but look more like bottlenose dolphins. Although they live in tropical and sub-tropical waters all over the world, most of their lifestyle remains mysterious. Even the function of the tiny grooves on their teeth, from which they get their name, has yet to be explained.

Common Characteristics

Dolphins that live in oceanic waters share many characteristics. Most species have bold color patterns shared by both males and females; most live in large schools; and many regularly mix with other dolphin species. To understand why they share these characteristics, you need to visualize them in their element.

If you watch a snorkeller who has jumped from a boat into clear oceanic waters, the first thing he does, whilst treading water, is put his head under and look down into the blueyblackness below him, then look in front, then to his sides and finally swivel round to check behind. The feeling is one of total vulnerability, for whilst you can see a long way in all directions, you are also visible to other creatures from all directions. Like standing alone in the middle of the African plains, there is nowhere to hide. It is just the same for the oceanic dolphins. From dawn to dusk, they live in full view of their predators: sharks, killer, false killer, pygmy killer and pilot whales, and just like the herbivores and lions on an Africa plain, no amount of

Through the looking glass. Nestled under the bow of a ship these dolphins peer back up at the photographer whilst jostling for the best position for a free ride. A habit probably acquired from racing in front of large whales, most species surf the underwater pressure waves in front of ships and boats. Such capers offer fantastic opportunities for close-up views of little-known species like these rough-toothed dolphins. Made distinctive by their angular dorsal fins, pale jaws and conical heads, such a view of these elusive animals is a rare treat.

camouflage will conceal them. Instead, like zebra, dolphins have adopted three strategies to survive.

The first is to stick together. Being with others means that there are more of you to spot a predator and the chances of you being the one to get eaten are reduced. If you have a partner, your chances of becoming dinner are halved, whilst if you are one in a thousand, the risk falls accordingly. But there are additional advantages to sticking together, as well as reducing the time it takes to be picked off by your predators.

With camouflage being of no use, body colors can be extended to act as cues for neighbors in the school. Bold patterns make it easier for an animal to understand the orientation and speed of those around it, and so when a predator makes a strike, one dolphin may spot it and move so that it is pointing away. Instantly its color pattern will look different from its neighbors and so they will change too. Consequently, information can pass across the whole school faster than the predator can swim and so the whole mass can maneuver safely around the predator's attack, just as a shoal of fish or a flock of birds wheels around and past a lunging barracuda or a swooping falcon. The predator has lost its element of surprise and as groups become larger this effect becomes stronger, until very large groups become almost immune to such attacks.

As a result, predators must adopt another approach. They single out animals in a school, herd, group, shoal or flock and pursue them until their victim tires or makes a mistake. Lions will lazily trail a herd of zebra until they spot a weak individual and then focus their attack on it. The key to avoiding being eaten, then, is to not allow yourself to be singled out. And this is the dolphins' third strategy. By each looking identical to their neighbors, they cannot be targeted. Instead, with each turn of the school, the chosen individual is lost in the mass and the attacker must choose again and again and again until it gives up.

Although schools of dolphins are made up of individuals, by swimming with each other, locking their movements together and by looking like one another, they improve their chances of survival in their transparent world. But what of the exceptions? Bottlenose, rough-toothed and Risso's dolphins often swim in small schools, have weak body patterning and have scars that make one individual look different from another. The exceptions, it seems, do prove the rule, because these three are the largest of the oceanic dolphins and may be too big to be attacked by ocean-going sharks or killer whales. In a similar way, one might expect the mixed schools of dolphins to allow predators to single-out animals; if a common dolphin were surrounded by striped dolphins it could easily be targeted. But here again the strategy holds up; a closer examination of these mixed schools reveals that within them there is segregation, with species swimming alongside their own kind.

But life in the oceans is not only about avoiding predation. Dolphins must breed, and in order to do so, males must advertize themselves. In most animals, the sexes look quite different. Picture male and female ducks, lions and peacocks; the males tend to be more brightly or more extravagantly colored, or grander, than the females. But looking different in the eyes of your own species will have its costs if you can be singled out by your predators. In dolphins, what sexual differences there are turn out to be subtle. Males may be a slightly different size or shape. In some forms of spinner dolphin, for instance, males grow a dorsal fin that tilts forward rather than back, as if it were put on the wrong way round, and develop a bulge on the underside of their body just in front of the tail flukes. In most other species the differences are even more subtle, if present at all. Instead, male dolphins maintain a behavioral repertoire that can be quickly extinguished if a predator arrives on the scene. The penises of male dolphins are usually hidden in folds of skin on their bellies, but can be extended at will and so may be used as a temporary signal of their sex to other animals. Male

dolphins also form bonds with other males and coordinate their behavior with such precision that they can appear mirror images of one another. Finally, males may also use specific calls to signal their sex and intentions.

Like breeding, the best methods to catch food may contrast with the best strategies needed to avoid being eaten yourself. If food is scarce then crowding together into groups of a thousand or more would lead to competition. But the constraints of living in the open oceans act in just the same way on fish and squid as they do on dolphins and so they also aggregate, providing massive food patches for the dolphins.

Life for dolphins in the open oceans places considerable pressures on them and many of the features that distinguish them from coastal or river dolphins are a direct result. However, as an ecological group, oceanic dolphins are incredibly successful animals and are without doubt the most abundant dolphins on earth. Indeed, the natural world can provide few rivals to the sheer visual impact of seeing a school of hundreds of oceanic dolphins powering through the waves.

Interactions with Man

One might imagine that oceanic dolphins, living where they do, could spend their lives as unaware of humans as we are of them. Whilst possibly true for a few populations in the southernmost oceans, this is certainly not the case for the rest. Some encounters between man and oceanic dolphin are inconsequential and brief – perhaps a few minutes riding the pressure wave in front of a sailing boat or tanker, or a game with floating rubbish. Some encounters may deeply influence the people experiencing them; a brief moment with spinner dolphins off Hawaii, or common dolphins off the Azores, can produce cherished memories. But for many dolphins, encounters with humans profoundly alter their lives for the worse.

The most significant interactions have involved our fisheries, and the most direct have been those aimed at the dolphins themselves. In many parts of the world, dolphins are intentionally netted, shot, harpooned or driven ashore for slaughter. In St Vincent and St Lucia in the Caribbean, rough-toothed, spinner, spotted, Clymene and other dolphins are harpooned from small boats and their flesh eaten. In the Black Sea recent hunts have taken a considerable toll on the populations of common dolphins. In Japan, hunts have been carried out to reduce local dolphin populations and so minimize perceived competition over dwindling fish stocks, whilst in the 1950s and 1970s, the French navy killed dolphins to reduce the damage to fishing nets. Most local hunts of these types go unrecorded and so their true impact is unknown.

Less visible, but more devastating, have been the unintentional fisheries for dolphins, of which driftnetting has been amongst the most publicized. Every night, across many oceans, thousands of miles of net are set to drift in the currents. During the swordfish season in the Mediterranean, for example, enough nets are set each night that if put end to end they would stretch from Spain in the west to Turkey in the east and back again. After a night at sea, the nets are retrieved and their catch recovered. Whilst aimed at commercially valuable fish, the nets make no distinction about what they catch and remove everything big enough to be entangled. Sharks, turtles, sea birds, seals, whales and dolphins are all caught in these 'walls of death'. In one, thankfully discontinued, Japanese fishery, a catch which netted 909 skipjack tuna also killed 97 dolphins and 11 whales. Removing this 'by-catch' from nets takes the fishermen time and means that more net repairing is required, but aside from this, has little effect on the fishery. The oceans, however, are methodically and wastefully sieved of their life. For example, the Japanese, Taiwanese and South Korean squid driftnet fleets in the North Pacific are thought to have depleted the population of northern right whale dolphins to between one-quarter and three-quarters of its former size. In view of such appalling statistics, the United Nations implemented a resolution in 1992 to ban large-scale high-seas driftnetting. This ban made illegal the use of the huge nets, and many driftnet fisheries were forced to close. But several have continued despite the ban and the legal use of shorter nets also continues.

An alternative solution to reduce by-catch has been to make the nets more selective. One way of doing this is to hang electronic devices ('pingers') on the nets which beep or make pinging noises, and so make the nets more obvious to marine mammals. But solving a fishery problem by quick-fix gear design like this is never as simple as it might appear. Pingers, for example, are the latest in a succession of ideas to keep dolphins, whales and porpoises from becoming entangled in fishing nets. Previous ideas have included gaps in the middle or top of nets ('dolphin doors') to allow the animals a chance to swim through or over. Another has been to hang fist-sized air-filled beads ('cat's eyes') all over the net to reflect the echolocation calls of dolphins and so indicate the net's presence. As electronic pingers have followed in the footsteps of many other abandoned ideas they have been treated with both scepticism and enthusiasm. However, so serious are the levels of cetacean by-catch in some areas that there is little choice but to find a viable solution or close the fisheries altogether.

One such case involves the lucrative bottom-set gill net fisheries off the eastern coast of the US and Canada, where harbor porpoises have been accidentally caught in such high numbers that their populations are under threat. The use of pingers seems like an ideal solution and there were many calls to fit them to the nets so that the fishery could continue. However, without proof that the devices reduced the numbers of porpoises caught, their implementation would simply be cosmetic. So a massive and ingeniously constructed trial was designed. In it an experimental fishery was set up and every net fitted with

pingers that were each a little smaller than a beer can. The devices were also specially built with switches that only turned them on when they were submerged below the water, thus the fishermen couldn't hear any beeping noises when they handled the nets. Furthermore only half of the pingers actually worked, the rest appeared identical but produced no noise. As well as the fishermen, each boat also carried an observer whose job was to count how many porpoises were caught. The beauty of the experiment was that neither the fishermen nor the observers knew which nets had the working pingers and which had the duds.

The results were astonishing: two porpoises were caught in the nets with pingers and 25 in the ones with duds. The devices clearly worked. But did this end the problem? The answer appears to be maybe. If the pingers work by scaring porpoises away from the vicinity of the nets then the animals will be excluded from the very places in which they need to feed. On the other hand, if the porpoises get used to the new noises, then the numbers caught in the nets are likely to creep back up to the original levels. Or even worse, if porpoises and other marine mammals feed on fish actually caught in nets then soon the animals will learn that the sound of pingers means dinner and the numbers caught will end up higher than they ever were before. Clearly such devices need long-term appraisal before they can be used safely.

The tuna fishery in the eastern tropical Pacific is another example of how complex solving fisheries problems can be. It is the world's most important tuna fishing area, where about a quarter of the total tuna catch is taken. Of the different species, the yellowfin tuna is the most economically important. As described earlier, these fish form an association with dolphins, particularly the spotted and spinners, so that finding dolphins often means finding tuna. Since the late 1950s fishermen have taken advantage of this association and caught tuna

*The right whale dolphins are the only oceanic dolphins without dorsal fins. Two species exist,
one in the north Pacific, the other (pictured here) in the southern oceans. The tuxedo color patterns
of these fast-swimming slender dolphins make them look more like huge penguins than dolphins.*

by finding a dolphin school, then setting a net to encompass it, and drawing it in until the tuna below can be captured. 'Setting on dolphins', as it is known, is the most effective way of catching the large and valuable yellowfin tuna. But this method has inflicted an enormous toll on the dolphins because many have been entangled and asphyxiated in the nets during the capture process.

The number of dolphins killed during the 1950s, 60s, and early 70s is unknown, but over 100,000 are thought to have been killed each year by US-registered boats alone. As these made up the majority of this fishing fleet at the time, the US National Marine Fisheries Service drew up regulations to reduce dolphin mortality. These included measures to ensure that nets and methods were modified so that dolphins could escape. Observers were also carried on board to ensure that the correct procedures were used and that the dolphins killed were counted. However, in the 1980s many of the US boats moved out of the area or changed to flags of other countries, while the fleets of many Latin American countries expanded. Management of this international fishery increasingly fell to the Inter-American Tropical Tuna Commission, who placed observers aboard all boats setting on dolphins. In addition, large amounts of research have been carried out, the fishing methods refined and political willpower and lobbying brought to bear.

Consequently the number of dolphins killed by all nationalities in the eastern tropical Pacific has fallen rapidly from over 130,000 a year in 1986 to 2500 in 1996. But whilst the number of dolphins being killed has been reduced, so has the size of the remaining stocks. In 1993, the US determined that two stocks were significantly depleted – the northeastern spotted dolphin population having declined by three-quarters and the eastern spinners by two-thirds.

While the current numbers of dolphins killed in this fishery are thought to be small enough to no longer threaten the future of their populations, it is unclear when or indeed if the populations will ever fully recover. Additionally, having thousands of dolphins die in nets each year continues to be a considerable welfare issue. But attempting to further reduce the number killed presents a difficult problem. Setting on dolphins means that adult tuna are caught, rather than the small and immature fish, which are the target of other methods. In terms of tuna conservation, then, setting on dolphins is preferred.

Different methods of catching tuna are detrimental to other marine life. Tuna also swim below floating logs and other debris, for unknown reasons, and setting nets around such flotsam can be a rewarding fishing practice. However, for the equivalent catch of marketable tuna, using this method, rather than setting on dolphins, for every dolphin saved over 16,000 undersized tunas, mahi-mahi, billfish and other large fishes, 21 sharks and rays, 1200 trigger and other small fishes, as well as sea turtles, are killed. Clearly, setting on dolphins cannot be banned in favor of these other methods. Instead, alternative ways of reducing the number of dolphins killed would need to be developed, but these are hampered by the lack of knowledge about both dolphins and tuna. If, for example, the bond between them were better understood, then perhaps methods of breaking it just prior to a set could be devised. But answering such questions may take decades of investigation, and research projects at sea are notoriously expensive and difficult.

Despite the impacts on dolphins by the tuna-fishing industry, we now know more about the dolphins of the eastern tropical Pacific than about those in any other ocean, and enough about their numbers to assess whether these impacts are critical to their populations. The spur for much of the investigations, changes in fishing practice and government strategy has come from public pressure. If we are to halt the process of the world's open oceans becoming empty oceans, then each of us must add our own weight to this pressure.

Like these Atlantic spotted dolphins, several oceanic species use coastal areas near their night-time deep-water feeding grounds to shelter and socialize during the day. They often pick shallow areas with a bright sandy bottom so that predatory sharks cannot sneak in below undetected.

Coastal Dolphins

A Coastal Dolphin's World

Imagine yourself as an eagle. You are perched on the ridge of a hill that continues to the horizon on either side of you; while in front, the ground gradually descends, reaching a flat plain in the far distance. The slope has small valleys of its own, rock out-crops and is paved with thickets of vegetation, while the plain beyond is barren and muddy. Everywhere you look, there are animals; they cling to the ground, scuttle amongst the rocks and flit between the patches of vegetation. Further out, huge flocks of prey wheel and dive, pursued by other eagles like yourself. Just above your head swirls the base of a cloud layer that stretches over this whole scene like a ceiling. A tenacious wind buffets this landscape, flattening the vegetation, lifting dust clouds and building up piles of sand and gravel. The wind has blown like this for the last six hours but at any moment will switch to blow just as hard from the opposite direction. You take flight to join the other eagles, away from the hillside and over the plain. The ground below continues for many miles but then suddenly ends with a precipitous cliff face with whatever lies at its base being far out of sight below. An icy updraft swirls up and over this edge and carries with it fine dust that attracts huge flocks of your prey.

Picture this scene, but swap the air for water, cloud-base for water-surface and wind for tides and you can begin to imagine the home of the coastal dolphins. They live throughout the coastal marine zone from where the waves chew at the land, across the continental shelf (our hillside and plain) to the continental edge where the seabed dives from 650 ft (200 m) below the surface into the oceanic abyss over 13,000 ft (400 m) below. The 13 species of dolphin that live in these waters are as varied as the scenery itself.

The Species

At the oceanic edge of the continental shelf, upcurrents and eddies bring nutrient-rich waters from the cold depths to the warm and brightly lit surface. Here plankton flourish and support a voracious food chain and many of the oceanic dolphins like the common, Risso's, spinner and striped dolphins come to feast. But this area is also used by coastal dolphins.

In the north Atlantic, between the British Isles and Norway, New England and Greenland, white-beaked dolphins occur. They feed in coastal areas right up to the shore and even in harbor mouths, but tend to congregate around the shelf edge. Like many coastal dolphins, they are generalist feeders and take flat fish and shrimps from the seabed as well as fish like herring from the water near the surface. These heavily built dolphins grow up to 10 ft (3 m) long and are black with chalky white patches on their sides, tail, and over their blunt heads and beaks. White-beaks are found in schools from just a few individuals up to many hundreds and can be acrobatic and boisterous around boats. Atlantic white-sided dolphins are very similar; they also live in the north Atlantic and feed over the continental shelf and its edge. Brief sightings at sea can lead to confusion with white-beaked dolphins but white-sided are about 18 in (0.5 m) shorter and their color patterns are more distinct, with dark backs, gray flanks and a white belly. Superimposed on this color pattern is a discrete patch of white on the flank below the dorsal fin and a tan-colored patch towards the tail.

Dusky dolphins are the southern hemisphere's equivalents of the north Atlantic's white-sided and white-beaked dolphins. Although closely related, duskys are about three-quarters of the length – 6 ft (1.9 m) – and are entirely black and white. These gregarious dolphins live around the coasts of South

America, South Africa, New Zealand and scattered islands in the southern Indian Ocean. A characteristic of coastal dolphins is their adaptability and dusky dolphins are a prime example. Off Argentina, small groups of eight to ten individuals spend their nights resting near shore, whilst during the day they search for schooling anchovies in the rich and shallow coastal waters. Upon finding fish, these duskys co-operate to drive them into a tight mass at the surface and then feed on them. Other groups will join in until two hundred or more dolphins may be feasting. Feeding is followed by a period of social activity before these super-groups split up for the night's resting. In contrast, dusky dolphins off New Zealand spend their entire day and night in compact groups of two or three hundred animals. Like Hawaiian spinner dolphins these duskys feed over the oceanic depths on animals in the deep scattering layer which rises towards the surface at night. During the day, this layer is too deep to reach and so the dolphins rest close to shore. Consequently, the New Zealand dolphins' activity patterns are almost the direct opposite to those of their Argentinean cousins.

Peale's dolphins live at the very southern tip of South America and around the Falkland (Malvinas) Islands and so share part of their range with the adaptable dusky dolphins. They have similar, if a little more muted, black and white color patterns, but are made distinctive by having dark faces (beak, melon and cheeks). Little is known about them, but they have been seen in coastal areas from the shelf edge to the shore line and even inshore of seaweed beds where octopus may be part of their otherwise unknown diet.

The coastal waters of the southern hemisphere are also host to four species of small plump dolphin (the Heaviside's, Chilean, Hector's and Commerson's) that have been placed together in an evolutionary genus called *Cephalorhynchus*. Whilst closely related to most other dolphins, they have ways of life and features that are more like those of the distantly related porpoises. Unlike most other dolphins, but like porpoises, the females grow larger than the males, both sexes have peculiar pimples along the leading edge of their fins and they produce very high-pitched echolocation calls. What makes these similarities even more intriguing (particularly for the pimples and the calls) is that nobody is absolutely sure what either the dolphins or the porpoises use them for. What is clear is that because both groups have evolved them independently, they must somehow be important for a *Cephalorhynchus*/porpoise way of life.

Of the four species, the Commerson's dolphin has the largest range, being found around the south-east coast of South America and the Falkland Islands. But what makes their range large is that they are also found off Kerguelen Island, which is 5300 miles (8500 km) to the east, in the southern Indian Ocean. Surprisingly, however, they are not found off southern Africa or around any of the islands in-between and one has to wonder how these coastal dolphins got to the isolated Kerguelen Island. Commerson's are small dolphins growing to 4 ft 3 in (1.3 m) long off South America and 5 ft 6 in (1.7 m) off Kerguelen Island. They have a thick and stocky body, rounded dorsal fin and blunt head. Their extremities — the head, tail, dorsal fin and pectoral flippers — are black whilst the rest of their skin is pure white. Commerson's inhabit nearshore waters of open coasts, sheltered fjords, bays, harbors and river mouths where they feed on small fish, squid, cuttlefish, several types of crustacean like crabs and krill and other invertebrates including brittle stars and sea squirts. They are energetic little dolphins and frequently leap, harass seagulls, investigate swimmers, surf on breaking waves and have the unusual habit of swimming and feeding whilst upside-down.

Commerson's live on the east coast of South America, Chilean dolphins live on the west, between northern Chile and Cape Horn. Although only a handful have been examined, they

Four coastal dolphin species.

Commerson's dolphins

Hector's dolphin

White-beaked dolphins

Atlantic white-sided dolphins

appear to grow to about the same size as the Commerson's and are a similar shape, but have an entirely different coloration pattern, being essentially gray with a white belly. They also have a dark crescent that runs from behind the blowhole to above the eye and a dark band on the belly between the pectoral flippers. This dolphin has most often been seen in shallow waters, but its precise habitat preferences, like its diet, are little known.

Heaviside's dolphins live only off the west coast of South Africa, Namibia and perhaps Angola. Their name comes from Captain Haviside, who was a ship's captain and probably carried the first specimen to England, where it was sold in 1828 to the Royal College of Surgeons. At about the same time, an eminent surgeon with a similar name but different spelling, Captain Heaviside, sold his collection of animal specimens. Through either a typographical error or a mistaken identity the two names got mixed up and to this day these dolphins are named after the wrong person. It was another 160 years before the actual living appearance of the dolphin was published.

Heaviside's dolphins are small and stocky and grow to about 5 ft 6 in (1.7 m) long. Most of their skin is blue-black, but between the head and the middle of the belly is a panel of gray. There is also a complex white area on the belly that forms a backward-pointing trident pattern. The eye is highlighted by a blue-black patch on the gray side panel and the dorsal fin is triangular. Totally white Heaviside's dolphins are occasionally seen, and some have olive-colored patches on their skin as a result of algae hitching a ride. They show a strong preference for shallow water, generally less than 330 ft (100 m) deep, probably because they feed on bottom-dwelling organisms like octopus, hake and gobies. They also associate in small groups up to a maximum of thirty, but are most often alone or in pairs or trios.

The final member of the *Cephalorhynchus* genus is the Hector's dolphin. These live only around the coast of New Zealand, particularly around South Island. Like the other members of the genus, Hector's are chubby little dolphins with short rotund bodies, up to 5 ft (1.5 m) long. They have disproportionately large tail flukes and pectoral flippers and a rounded dorsal fin which looks uncannily like one of Mickey Mouse's ears. Whilst their bodies are predominantly gray, the belly is creamy-white from the snout to nearly as far as the tail but branches with a finger-like extension on to each flank. The tail, dorsal fin, flippers and side of the head are black. Like the Chilean dolphins, which live on the other side of the Pacific Ocean, they also have a black crescent running from the blow-hole to just above the eye. The behavioral repertoire of Hector's dolphins appears to be plentiful with bubble-blowing, leaping, tail-slapping, spy-hopping, surfing, playing with floating objects, group leaping and body contact between dolphins being observed. Hector's are often found in small groups of two to eight individuals and these frequently come together, merge and split. They feed on bottom-living and free-swimming prey including mullet and squid and occasionally follow trawlers, apparently feeding on the fish stirred up by the fishing net.

Another coastal dolphin that may be closely related to the *Cephalorhynchus* genus has turned feeding behind trawlers into an art. Humpback dolphins live around tropical coasts from western Africa to South Africa, the Middle East to India, Malaysia to southern China and Borneo to north and eastern Australia. Throughout this large and near-shore range, humpback dolphins vary considerably in both body shape and body color and consequently many researchers feel that there are actually several species of humpback dolphin. However, the number is disputed. 'Splitters' recognize five species, 'lumpers'

Hector's dolphins are found only in the coastal waters off New Zealand. They prefer shallow waters within a few miles of the shore.

put them into just two; the Atlantic and the Indo-Pacific forms. To confuse matters even further, recent evidence suggests that there is actually only one species!

All humpback dolphins are robust in form and, unusually for dolphins, their bodies are deeper than they are broad. They grow up to 9 ft (2.8 m) long and have a long thin beak that makes up about a tenth of their body length. Their flippers and tail flukes are large and broad, and their dorsal fin and back give them their most distinctive feature. Humpback dolphins from South Africa have a ridge that runs along the top of their backs, over nearly 40% of their length; in its middle, there is a small and pointed dorsal fin. Humpback dolphins living in the western Pacific have a less marked dorsal ridge and a large triangular dorsal fin. Like their shape, their colors also vary between populations. In the Atlantic they are slate-gray on the back and sides and a little paler on the belly, and adults may be flecked with dark spots. Dolphins in the northern Indian Ocean are uniformly lead- or brownish-gray, whilst in Chinese waters, adults are pink or white from one end of their bodies to the other and may have a dark eye-patch and dark blotches scattered over them. Animals living further south, off eastern Australia, however, are colored gray, much like their Atlantic counterparts.

Humpback dolphins are totally coastal and rarely venture into waters deeper than 70 ft (20 m). Instead, they make shallow-water living their forté and use rising tides to penetrate river deltas, tidal creeks and mangrove swamps where they feed on bottom- or shore-living fish and avoid the attentions of sharks. In many parts of their range humpback dolphins make a living by following trawlers. These boats drag nets across the bottom, stirring up fish and prawns before they are overtaken by the net. But some flee to the sides or slip through the mesh and the dolphins position themselves to intercept them. The dolphins have also learnt to take fish discarded from the boats after the nets have been landed. These new methods of feeding

have proved highly profitable to many populations and in several parts of their range, like the waters around urban Hong Kong, the best way to find these dolphins is to look for a working trawler. When feeding around the boats, humpback dolphins can form groups of fifteen or more animals, but more normally they swim on their own or in groups of two to five. In parts of eastern Australia, feeding around trawlers brings humpback dolphins into close contact with bottlenose dolphins which are up to the same tricks.

Although bottlenose dolphins were introduced in the Oceanic Dolphins section, they are also very much coastal dolphins and can be found everywhere from the clear and open waters at the continental shelf edge to murky inshore mangrove swamps. In fact, bottlenose dolphins can be found in any temperate, sub-tropical or tropical marine water from Nova Scotia (Canada) to Cape Town (South Africa), Madagascar to Christchurch (New Zealand) and Tokyo (Japan) to Valparaiso (Chile), making them the most widespread dolphins of all. In consequence, they are the best known and their sheer adaptability has also meant that they survive in habitats as artificial as busy industrial harbors or indoor aquaria.

Bottlenose dolphins are generally gray, being slightly darker on the back and paler below. They have a distinct blunt beak and tall sickle-shaped fin. After this, little is constant. Bottlenose dolphins in the tropical waters off western Australia reach barely 6 ft 6 in (2 m) long at maturity, whilst in the chilled waters of northern Scotland they grow to 11 ft 6 in (3.5 m) and weigh perhaps three times as much as their warm-water cousins. Bottlenose dolphins off Florida may never dive to depths of more than 30 ft (10 m) in their whole lives, whilst off the coast of Croatia they frequently dive to 165 ft (50 m) and more. Around islands west of the French coast, they live in close-knit groups that rarely stray more than a few miles from their favored spot, whilst just over the horizon off the English coast,

A case of mistaken identity? Humpback dolphins have a coastal range from western Africa, through Asia to eastern Australia and across which they vary markedly in color. Humpback dolphins in Chinese waters, like those above, begin life a lead-gray and develop spots of pink that cover their whole bodies in adulthood. In contrast, dolphins in the Atlantic are gray and adults gain some dark spots as they age. These and other regional differences have led to arguments about how many species of humpback dolphin there actually are. Some propose as many as five whilst others maintain only one. The jury is still out.

other bottlenose dolphins wander continuously along hundreds of miles of coastline. Newborn bottlenose dolphins off Florida retain the pale creases on their skin from being enfolded in the womb for about three months, whilst off Scotland they are kept for 18 or more months.

Whichever feature you pick, it seems, it will vary from one population to the next. To complement this, they have large brains and have developed many ingenious ways to survive. Off western Australia they have worked out how to untie the fishermen's knots at the end of trawling nets and so help themselves to the whole catch; off South Carolina and western Australia they have learnt to chase fish on to muddy shores and then beach themselves to pick them up; off Brazil and Mauritania bottlenose dolphins have struck up a symbiotic relationship with coastal fishermen so that they can catch mullet together; and in several areas they appear to use tools to achieve their desires. For example, two captive bottlenose dolphins were observed attempting to dislodge a moray eel from a crevice. After many attempts, one dolphin went off and found a scorpion fish, carried it to the crevice and poked at the eel with the spiny fish. The eel then abandoned the crevice and was caught by the dolphin. Wild bottlenose dolphins off western Australia also appear to use tools, but instead of fish they use sponges, but what they are used for, nobody knows.

Irrawaddy dolphins also feed around trawlers and can be found in coastal areas from the Bay of Bengal to northern Australia. They have also taken up residence in several major river systems that discharge into their coastal range. They grow to about 8 ft 10 in (2.7 m) long and have rounded heads without a distinct beak. Their flippers are large, but their dorsal fin is small and set far back on their gray or slate-blue bodies. Although social they rarely form groups larger than fifteen, six or fewer being more common.

Tucuxi dolphins have a similar way of life, living in coastal areas and venturing into neighboring rivers. Their range stretches between Brazil and Panama on the north-eastern tip of South America. Overall, tucuxi look like bottlenose dolphins, but are smaller, about 6 ft (1.9 m) long, having a rather stubby body, a distinct beak and a triangular dorsal fin. Their backs are lead-gray or brown gradually paling to cream or pink on the belly. Their diet in coastal waters is little known but they form groups of up to 25 or so individuals.

The final coastal dolphin is the most unusual. The franciscana belongs to a group of dolphins called the Platanistidae, of which all other members live in rivers. As the franciscana lives in coastal marine waters between Argentina and Brazil in eastern South America, it is the odd one out in this group. They grow up to 5 ft 6 in (1.7 m) long but are actually tiny dolphins because a fifth of this length is made up by their beaks which protrude in front of them like enormous forceps and are festooned with more than two hundred teeth. Behind this, their heads are domed and their bodies gray. They have broad pectoral flippers and tail flukes and a triangular dorsal fin. Like humpback dolphins, of which they appear to be the South American equivalent, franciscana live only in waters fringing the coast and tend to prefer water of 30 ft (10 m) or less where they feed on small bottom-living fish, squid and shrimps.

Common Characteristics

The dolphins that live in coastal waters encompass a variety of features. There are brightly colored species and ones with dull skins, robust dolphins and delicate sinuous ones, highly sociable members and others that are almost solitary. But this spectrum of possibilities is far from random; instead these characteristics are directly matched with the nature of the coastal habitat in which each lives.

Just as the white-beaked and Atlantic white-sided dolphins

share the edge of the continental shelf with oceanic representatives like common and striped dolphins, so this habitat shares its characteristics with the open oceans. Clear and unrestricted water means nowhere to hide for dolphins pursued by predators and so they need counter-measures. Large schools dilute and confuse the pressure from attacking sharks and killer whales whilst their distinctive color patterns help them co-ordinate fast avoidance measures with split-second timing. To catch their mobile prey, dolphins in clear waters must also be fast swimmers and so, like their oceanic neighbors, are built like muscular torpedoes, with robust beaks, stout bodies and narrow flippers, fins and flukes.

Further inshore, the seabed rises within reach of wave action and tidal currents. These forces reduce the underwater visibility by lifting sediment into the water, in combination with run-off from the land, and they also carry nutrients to the surface and plankton begin to bloom. The water is turned cloudy green by their pigments and vision becomes less and less important to either predators or prey. Dolphins do not need to form big schools as simply fleeing in this foggy world is enough to escape predators. But the dolphins' prey also gain shelter in the murky water and form smaller groups of their own. This gives dolphins like the humpback, Peale's and Irrawaddy another reason to form small schools, otherwise they would end up competing with their schoolmates every time they found prey.

The co-ordinated behavior of the Argentinean dusky dolphins is an alternative strategy, whereby they can round up clumps of fish, big enough to feed a large group. In so doing, the number of members in their schools increases when they find abundant fish and then falls at the end of the day after feeding. Bottlenose and Hector's dolphins also employ this strategy, but instead of being fixed into a daily routine of groups merging and then splitting, they do so continuously as they come across different-sized patches of food. These conditions lead to what are known as 'fission-fusion' societies. Consequently, all the members living in a particular area may interact while feeding and so each dolphin will have many associates with which it needs to have some kind of a relationship. Just remembering all of these individuals is one of the reasons that coastal dolphins, particularly the bottlenose dolphin, are thought to need such large brains.

Of course, in restricted visibility, hiding from predators is possible and so the dolphins that live in these waters, like the tucuxi, bottlenose, Chilean and (Atlantic) humpback dolphins have muted colors to blend in with their surroundings. In areas of extremely low visibility, vision is of no use at all to anything and so dolphins like the franciscana and Chinese humpback dolphins have skin with little, if any, pigment. Living in totally opaque water means that other senses are needed to find food and avoid predators; while dolphins have the fantastic advantage of being able to switch on their echolocation sense to visualize their surroundings, and the franciscana and humpback dolphins also use their long forceps-like beaks to probe the muddy bottom.

Like the visibility, habitat complexity also tends to change across the coastal fringe. In waters at the edge of the continental shelf, far from land, the habitat is sufficiently uniform that swimming in one direction for more than a minute or two will make little difference. In contrast, close inshore the surroundings are far more complex. Swimming straight for more than a few seconds in a mangrove swamp or tidal channel would end in disaster. In consequence, the dolphins that live furthest inshore tend to be more flexible and have larger flippers, fins and flukes than their offshore equivalents and this allows them to maneuver in confined spaces. Perhaps this is one reason why most inshore species appear to fare much better in captivity than their offshore relatives.

A jump for joy? Dolphins of all species leap out of the water, but it is unclear why they do it. Fast swimmers make long low jumps to get a breath free from spray, but animals like this dusky dolphin will leap vertically to re-enter where it left. Such breaches may help catch fish or, by making distinctive splashes, have social functions. Alternatively they may give the dolphin a chance to look around above the water or simply be an extension of other underwater antics.

Water babies: two bottlenose dolphin calves surface in the sheltered waters of a coastal estuary. Whilst living close to land offers them protection from rough seas and provides spectacular views for shore-based dolphin watching, this proximity also brings them into contact with other human activities. Runoff from the land brings agricultural, domestic and industrial pollutants into the food chain, channel and harbor dredging muddies the water and, coupled with shipping and boating, produces an underwater cacophony of noise for these animals with long-range and sensitive hearing.

Interactions with Man

Of all dolphins, it is those at the coasts that experience the widest range of human activities. They encounter all types of shipping and recreational boating, as well as petrochemical, sewage, pesticide, nuclear and noise pollution. They are harpooned, netted, driven ashore and struck by boats, blasted by dynamite, seismic bangs and military sonar. Their habitats are snipped away by land reclamation or dredging and their prey are taken by our fisheries or altered by our mismanagement. And now it seems that we must add climate change to this list.

Some dolphins are more vulnerable to specific threats than others. The Commerson's, Hector's, Chilean and Heaviside's dolphins seem to be particularly vulnerable to capture in bottom-set fishing nets whilst species like humpback and bottlenose dolphins may become addicted to our fickle fishing methods. But most worrying are the long-term threats and most widespread are those posed by chemical pollution, particularly the organochlorines, like DDT, dieldrin and the PCBs. These long-lived chemicals find their way from agricultural land, plastics manufacturing or electronic equipment into the seas from the air, sediments, river discharges, land-based food chains and direct spillages. They are taken up by small organisms including the plankton which are in turn eaten by larger and larger animals. Finally, at the crown of the food chain they are ingested by dolphins. Because most of these compounds can neither be broken down nor excreted from the animals in each link of this chain, they build up at each step. A shrimp may ingest a few thousand particles of pollutant and store them. A fish then eats a few thousand shrimps and stores their collected pollutants. A bigger fish eats this fish along with a few hundred others and so on up the chain to dolphins. A single dolphin may eat several hundred thousand fish in its lifetime and because it cannot discharge these artificial compounds they can build up to levels capable of poisoning its immune and reproductive

systems. With reduced immunity the abilities of dolphins to fight their normal diseases can be reduced and epidemics may break out or their whole lives can be altered by continual disease. Reproductive disruption is less visible, but, given time, can whittle away a population just as effectively.

Perhaps the most worrying aspect of these pollutants is the way in which they are passed from mother to offspring. Being only soluble in fat, they are stored in the dolphin's fat reserves, but when a female gives birth to her calf a dose of the pollutants that she has built up in previous years is given to the growing fetus. Then when it is born, it lives off her milk which itself comes from her fat stores. Thus the growing calf gets fed on toxic milk from the moment it is born and if it is her first calf, it receives up to 80% of the mother's accumulated store of pollutants. Many researchers fear that this toxic shot may be enough to kill her first calf; if it doesn't and the calf is female she herself will grow up to pass on her mother's and her own burden to her first calf. Clearly the problems of these extremely common pollutants are going to continue for many dolphin-generations to come, even after we have the sense to cease using these chemicals.

However, not all of our impacts on coastal dolphins are necessarily negative. By living in habitats easily accessible to humans, many coastal dolphins have offered us fantastic opportunities to get to know them. The most famous occasions are provided by the so-called 'sociable' dolphins that, for reasons known only to themselves, choose human company over that of other dolphins. These friendly but wild animals were first recorded by the ancient Greeks and have been a regular feature of coastal towns world-wide ever since. At any one time, there are usually two or three such dolphins scattered around the world. Single male or female bottlenose, common, dusky, Risso's, spinner and striped dolphins have all formed relationships with particular boats or people. Where they do, they often act like a magnet for folk wanting to swim with a dolphin, be healed of an ailment or simply spend time with a wild animal that also seeks their company. In areas where a sociable dolphin stays long enough to gain a reputation, it can provide a considerable input into the local economy with legions of tourists, film crews and journalists booking up the spare accommodation, filling the restaurants and hiring the local transport. The experiences that people have had with these dolphins are often profound and much has been written about them, but what it is that a dolphin gains by having hundreds or even thousands of people swimming with it each week is unknown. Rather sadly, surprisingly few people have ever made an effort to try and find out.

In Monkey Mia, off western Australia, a relationship has built up between a group of local people and a group of local bottlenose dolphins. Nowadays, the dolphins come close inshore to swim amongst a forest of legs as tourists stand in the water and offer them fish. The dolphins' visits appear to be by choice and seem to be driven by something other than hunger as they often visit the feeding beach but do not actually take any of the fish that they are offered. They also respond differently towards adults and children, familiar people and strangers. While swimming amongst the legs of up to a hundred thousand people a year the dolphins allow themselves to be petted and tickled, they accept or reject fish and also offer fish back in return. They beach themselves simply to watch the tourists staring back at them. Adult dolphins bring their calves to the beach too, as if to continue the tradition. What is actually going on in this extraordinary human-dolphin relationship is far from understood, but this small group of dolphins, which belongs to a larger population living further out in the same bay, has taught us much about the wider structuring of dolphin societies. Mothers bring their infants with them and so we have learnt that their feeding habits are passed from one generation to the next; pairs, trios or whole gangs of males follow habituated females into shore to try and mate with them; groups of males compete with one another over the females and finally, we have learnt that every individual dolphin, male or female, adult or calf, behaves quite differently to its associates.

Getting to know the differences between the individuals in a population of wild animals must be among the most rewarding facets of studying animal behavior. No longer is spending half an hour in the presence of a school simply that. Instead it can become a fascinating update on recent events like the latest episode in a soap opera. One essential requirement, however, is to be able to recognize one individual from another, and in recent years we have discovered that when you look closely at any school of dolphins there are almost always subtle differences in the appearance of the individuals. One may have a nick in the back of its dorsal fin, another a scar and another a slightly different shaped patch of color. Once you have recognized these differences then suddenly each dolphin becomes an individual and the soap-opera updates can begin. One of the problems, however, is that dolphins often move too quickly for us to see these marks and so researchers have to take photographs and work out who was who later. This technique, called 'photo-identification', has revolutionized studies of wild dolphins. The other essential facet of such work is that we can now get ourselves into the position to meet up the with same individuals over and over again. For dolphins that live far offshore, that track ocean currents or live in overgrown and murky rivers, meeting the same individuals more than once is impossible. But for species that stay within easily reachable localized or sheltered areas, repeated observations are far easier and for this reason the societies of wild coastal dolphins are becoming the best studied. With an understanding of how coastal dolphin societies function we can begin to make inferences about the more elusive species which live far out to sea or in the overgrown, sediment-laden waters of some of the world's great rivers.

River Dolphins

A River Dolphin's World

Imagine yourself in a network of pipes like the London or New York underground train systems. Now imagine that the tunnels are filled with fog so thick that the walls, floor, ceiling and even your hands and feet are invisible. The only faint light in the gloom comes from above. Not only is the fog completely opaque, but it is blowing through the tunnels with such force that you have to jog just to stay in the same spot. A great forest is growing above the tunnels and the trees have pushed their roots through the walls and floor, whilst fallen branches and trunks litter your path. Sandwiches, chocolate bars and other goodies are carried along through the debris by the gale. Where tunnels join, eddies form and with them small refuges from the wind; here too tasty morsels build up. There are others like you in these tunnels but they glide by invisibly.

Picture a life in this labyrinthine world and you can begin to imagine what it is like to be a member of one of the few dolphin species which spend their entire lives in the silt-laden waters of Asian and South American rivers. These are the river dolphins, possibly some of the most bizarre-looking, perhaps the most primitive but certainly the most endangered of any of the dolphins alive today.

The Species

The six dolphin species that occupy this special habitat have very different origins. One, the tucuxi, belongs to the family Delphinidae, as do most of the oceanic and coastal dolphin species. It lives in coastal waters between Brazil and Panama on the north-eastern tip of South America. Several major river systems open out in this area (principally the Orinoco and the Amazon) and populations of tucuxi have moved into them. In

taking up a freshwater existence they now venture almost to the base of the Andes, over 1500 miles (2500 km) inland. Overall, tucuxi look much like their delphinid relatives, particularly the bottlenose dolphin, but they are much smaller, about 4 to 6 ft (1.3 to 1.9 m) long, with a rather stubby body, a distinct beak and a triangular dorsal fin. Their backs are usually lead gray or brown in color and they gradually pale to cream or pink on the belly. Populations living in freshwater tend to be smaller and paler than populations of tucuxi that stayed in the sea and so it has been suggested that they may have started to develop into separate freshwater and marine species. But at present the differences between them are so slight that they are still considered races of the same species.

An entirely different species, the Irrawaddy dolphin, has taken up a similar coastal and freshwater existence. Its evolutionary history is difficult to reconstruct but it perhaps has its closest relatives in the beluga whale and the almost mythical narwhal with its 'unicorn'-like tusk. The beluga and the narwhal are inhabitants of the Arctic, and the Irrawaddy dolphin may be their equatorial equivalent. The Irrawaddy dolphin occurs in coastal areas between the Bay of Bengal and northern Australia. Like the tucuxi, they penetrate river systems that open out into their coastal range. These rivers include the Mahakam in Borneo, the Mekong in Vietnam, Cambodia and Lao PDR (formerly Laos), the Ganges and Brahmaputra in India and the Irrawaddy in Burma. Irrawaddy dolphins are larger than tucuxi, about 6 ft 10 in to 8 ft 10 in (2.1 to 2.7 m) long. Their heads are blunt and do not have a distinct beak. Their flippers are large and rounded, while their dorsal fin is small and set quite far back on the body. Like the tucuxi they lack stripes or color patches, and are gray or dark slate blue with a paler belly.

The remaining four species of river dolphins are highly specialized and never found in the sea. They belong to a cetacean family called the true river dolphins or the Platanistidae. This group was so called after the name given in a dictionary published in 200 BC by Pliny the Elder, a Greek historian, but sadly the actual meaning of this name has been lost. The true river dolphins are quite different in appearance to all other dolphin species except for the coastal franciscana, their only marine relative. The baiji are the rarest of the true river dolphins. They live only in China and furthermore only in one river system, the Yangtze. Historically, they ranged over 1000 miles (1700 km), from the sluggish estuarine river mouth to the faster flowing Three Gorges area, as well as the associated tributaries and lakes in between. But today, as a result of human activities, their range is much smaller.

The Brahmaputra River arises from the same mountain range as the Yangtze but instead drains south west into Bangladesh and eventually into the Bay of Bengal. Just before it reaches the sea it merges with the Ganges River which flows through India and Nepal. The Brahmaputra, the Ganges and the Meghna Rivers are all home to another river dolphin, the susu, so named after the in-out breathing sound that it makes when it surfaces for air. The susu has a very similar relative, the bhulan, which lives in the Indus River in Pakistan. In fact the bhulan is physically so similar to the susu that the two species are sometimes classified as one. However, because they are restricted to rivers geographically divided by the Indian subcontinent, interbreeding is impossible and so they can be safely regarded as biologically distinct from one another. The last of the four true river dolphins is the boto which shares much of its South American range with the freshwater populations of tucuxi. Botos live in rivers in Brazil, Bolivia, Colombia, Peru and Venezuela, principally the Amazon, Guaviare, Maranon, Orinoco and Negro and their tributaries. Like the tucuxi, botos penetrate deep into the South American land mass as far as the foothills of the Andes. But unlike the tucuxi, they are never found in the sea.

The platanistoids look very similar to one another and quite unlike any other dolphins. They don't have the sleek torpedo-like shape normal in oceanic and coastal dolphins. Instead their 6 ft 6 in- to 7 ft 6 in- (2- to 3 m-) long bodies are sinuous and lumpy. Much of this difference in appearance is produced by an unusual feature among dolphins, a neck. This allows the platanistoids to point their heads up, down and some way towards their sides. This unusual ability is afforded by the spinal vertebrae at the base of their skulls which are distinct and well articulated, unlike other dolphins, but like those in ourselves and most land mammals. Furthermore, their bodies lack the normally thick layers of muscle and blubber behind the skull and so allow them unimpeded head movements. Of course, a neck does little to promote a streamlined body shape, but for these dolphins, the value of being able to move the head freely must be more important.

In front of the neck comes the head which is also unusual. Their jaws are long and slender and in some baiji and susu they are distinctly upturned; making up a fifth of the body's length, they extend in front of the animal like a huge pair of forceps. What's more the jaws are festooned with as many as two hundred teeth. Like other dolphin species, each tooth is a conical peg but in the boto the enamel is wrinkled, giving the teeth a rough texture and brownish color. Furthermore, the teeth are not all the same size. In the susu and bhulan, they get longer towards the tip of the jaw and, unlike any other marine dolphin, they are not hidden when the mouth is closed but interlock on the outside of the jaw to form a fearsome-looking cage around the tip of the beak. Having such a toothy beak would seem like a useful adaptation for catching fish, so it is interesting that no marine dolphins expose their teeth like this. A clue as to why not might come from the beaked whales, a group of marine

Irrawaddy dolphins live in shallow coastal areas between southern India and
northern Australia. These dolphins can maneuver in confined river channels and tolerate both
fresh and saline water. This adaptability has meant that they have been able to be successfully kept
and bred in captivity. Their physical resemblance to two arctic cetaceans, the narwhal and beluga whales,
has led to them often being classified into the same evolutionary group. However, others argue
that Irrawaddy dolphins are more closely related to the other oceanic and coastal dolphins.

The temperature of tropical rivers may alter little through the year, but the amount of water that they carry can change dramatically. In the Amazon and Orinoco, for example, water levels can rise by as much as 46 ft (14 m) after heavy rains. For resident dolphins, like this tucuxi, such a rise presents a time of upheaval. Suddenly they can leave the old river channels and hunt for fish in small tributaries, new lakes and among the tree trunks of the flooded forest.

whales that have lost almost all of their teeth. Males, however have kept one pair which erupt from the lower jaw, forming tusks. But by being exposed, they also act as solid anchoring sites for parasitic barnacles which then dangle into the water like the tassels on a rug. The barnacles make a living by filtering food from the moving water and can grow to be 1 in (5 cm) or more long. As the beaked whales only have two exposed teeth, the hitchhiking barnacles can do little to impede the progress of the whale, but if marine dolphins were to expose their hundred or more teeth they could rapidly acquire a beard of barnacles which would destroy their streamlining and otherwise get in the way. Such barnacles are absent from the freshwater home of the river dolphins and so perhaps this explains why these dolphins can display their teeth. Whether this is the reason or not, the teeth of the susu and bhulan would be the envy of any dinosaur or alien invader.

Running along the length of the upper jaws above each row of teeth is a line of tiny hairs. Similar hairs are found in other dolphins but only in fetuses and newborn calves. At the point where the jaw meets the rest of the skull are the eyes, but not the big watery eyes of marine dolphins. Instead they are tiny, like shrivelled raisins. Vision can be of little value to these dolphins because in two species, the susu and bhulan, their eyes lack the lenses needed to focus an image. Above the eyes is the melon, the fatty body that gives dolphins their bulbous forehead and is thought to focus the sounds that they emit into beams. The platanistoids can deform the shape of their melon at will, using muscles inside the head, and probably alter the direction or frequency characteristics of their calls. Behind the neck is a sinuous body and a pair of huge paddle-like pectoral flippers which are both broad and long. Only the baiji and franciscana have a dorsal fin; the susu, bhulan and boto just have low dorsal humps or ridges. The peduncle, the area between the dorsal fin and tail flukes, is very short and in all species the tail flukes are broad, flexible and often rather tattered.

Most of the true river dolphins are shy creatures that swim slowly, roll gently at the surface when breathing and rarely lift their tail flukes above the water. However, when disturbed or socializing they are capable of turns of speed and can leap out of the water. River dolphins are notoriously difficult for researchers to follow in the wild because they often surface in one direction then quickly flip round underwater and swim the opposite way. Then, just before surfacing again, they turn once more and surface in the same direction as they began. They can also surface quietly without any audible blow and even then may only expose the tip of the melon and blowhole, not an eye-catching sight in a silty river with riffles, waves and floating debris. Underwater they can swim in a variety of orientations, and upside-down or side swimming is common. When they dive they rarely stay submerged for more than three minutes at a time.

The bhulan, susu and baiji dolphins are not brightly colored; instead each tends to be a uniform ash-white, gray, or brown, from belly to back depending on the species and habitat. Baijis, for example, are almost entirely white, leading to their common name which translates from Chinese as 'white flag dolphin'. In contrast, susu and bhulan are usually brown or gray. Their color may also change with their physical state. All live in warm waters and often generate too much heat. Sweating would be useless underwater so cetaceans divert their warmest blood to their skin, where it is cooled by the passing water. Normally, this process is invisible from the outside but dolphins with little or no pigment noticeably blush and when very warm they can turn completely pink! The color of botos is less indicative of their physical state as they are permanently bright pink or pinky gray.

Common Characteristics

It is evident that the true river dolphins are physically quite unlike most other dolphins, but they do share characteristics with the tucuxi and Irrawaddy dolphins. For instance, all have large pectoral flippers and muted colors. And like them, the Irrawaddy dolphin has a flexible neck, whilst the tucuxi has an extraordinarily long beak. Perhaps the tucuxi and Irrawaddy dolphins represent intermediates between fully marine dolphins and the highly specialized and extraordinary true river dolphins, all of whose adaptations are tuned to life in the complex, silty, confined, ever-changing freshwater environment in which they live.

Imagine yourself once again in the foggy, overgrown underground system. But go one stage further, and imagine that you are a marine dolphin swimming through this maze. Imagine also that you have a magical gift to change your body any way you want to help you survive. For a start you can't see anything but the faintest of shadows, so why go to the trouble of maintaining complicated eyes? Better just to keep a pair that would tell you whether it was day or night and concentrate your mind on more useful senses. Because of the gloom, nothing can see you either, so why not save resources by dispensing with the pigment required to maintain a complicated color pattern? Maneuvering around sunken tree roots and broken branches requires great care, so swimming with speed is rarely necessary. Rather than constrain yourself by being meticulously streamlined you would do better to have flippers and flukes that would allow you to swerve and curve, snake-like, around these obstacles. Big and broad flippers and flukes are best for slow and abrupt changes in direction. A dorsal fin would make swimming upside-down difficult, and would get bumped by floating wood on the surface, so that can be reduced or entirely lost as well.

The skin of marine dolphins is damaged by prolonged exposure to fresh water so your skin would need to become more resilient to low salt concentrations. Your food, those suspended chocolate bars and sandwiches mentioned earlier, would

actually be freshwater fish of as many as fifty different species. They teem in abundance in this rich habitat, but are particularly abundant where rivers join or channels merge. If these fish sense your presence they will immediately dart for cover in the sunken vegetation and so having a stubby head would be nearly useless for prising them out. However, jaws like long forceps would be ideal, particularly if you could maneuver them with dexterity, and so a mobile neck is an advantage. The forceps-like jaws and maneuverable neck combination would also be ideal for trawling through the bottom sediment and snapping up any hiding shrimps, crabs or freshwater turtles living there. As a young dolphin you would have had sensory hairs on your beak so that you could feel your mother's side when suckling. However, as your other senses became more adept the hairs were unnecessary and disappeared. But for the true river dolphins, grubbing about in the bottom in total darkness, probing your long snout into the semi-liquid mud, these hairs can be used to tell you when you are touching food and so they are retained.

Finally, with sight being an almost useless sense and touch only giving you information on what is immediately next to you, you'll need some form of early-warning system to tell you where your food is, where the obstacles lie and in fact whether you are in your home area or are too far up- or down-stream. Unsurprisingly, you would become very reliant on echolocation for navigation as well as hunting and maneuvering, and your mental map of the world would become an almost entirely acoustic one.

So, starting as a marine dolphin and by making just the simplest changes to your body to survive in a river, you could end up looking very much like one of the genuine river dolphins. And likewise, it is easy to see why the river dolphins are physically so unlike the marine dolphins. But they also differ in their behavior. In rivers there are many hiding places, so fish don't

Whilst young and light, botos can jump fully out of the water; adults
like these, however, lack sufficient propulsion and drag their bellies across the
surface. This is because they never have to contend with the large waves found in the sea
or pursue high-speed open water fish. Instead these dolphins are built for maneuverability
in confined river channels and undergrowth and can turn in their own lengths.

*The true river dolphins are unusual-looking creatures. Their long thin beaks may make
up a fifth of their body length and be armed with as many as 200 needle-like teeth. They have
tiny eyes, an articulated neck, large flippers, broad tail flukes and little or no dorsal fin.*

form great schools, tending to be solitary or found in small schools. Crustaceans and molluscs, too, will be scattered around in the environment. So, unlike the oceanic dolphins, there would be few advantages for river dolphins to swim in big groups because when food was found it would provide for only a few of them. They would then be left competing for the meal rather than benefiting from each other's presence.

The other force shaping social affiliation is predation. Where there are predators and no cover there is usually safety in numbers. But again the complexity of a riverine home offers the dolphins an abundance of shelter were a predator to launch an attack. In any case, river dolphins have few natural predators. For the boto, anacondas and caiman may offer a minor threat to young dolphins but rarely to adults, whilst the famed piranha fish is more likely to end up as a meal than be a menace. The baiji, bhulan and susu have few natural predators to fear. Consequently, river dolphins tend to be solitary or swim in groups of between two and six individuals and only occasionally form schools of up to sixteen or seventeen animals. The integrity of these groups is maintained by touch and whistles just as other dolphins do when out of visual contact.

Tropical rivers are quite unlike the sea in another respect. They can change radically in size with the seasons. In the dry season the flow is restricted to narrow channels but when the rains come, everything changes. Precipitation may occur many thousands of miles away, but almost overnight, the flow can increase by ten times, rising and spilling over the banks to flood the surrounding land. Suddenly the river dolphin's home becomes huge, like finding the escalator, then the exit from our foggy overgrown underground system. The dolphins can then range over the flooded land of grassy fields or dense forests. The fish, too, make an escape from the old river channel. The annual flood represents a time of upheaval for river dolphins and with it comes a change in their behavior. They tend to swim

in smaller groups and often head up-river to tap new and previously un-navigable channels. At the end of the wet season, the rivers shrink back to their former levels and the dolphins must find their way back to the river channels or they become trapped in drying lakes and pools.

There are many great rivers in the rest of Asia, Africa, Europe and North America and one wonders why dolphins have not colonized them. It is inconceivable that such rich waterways have remained undiscovered by dolphins. Bottlenose dolphins, for example, live in estuaries throughout the world and even swim into the parent river's lower reaches. I have watched common dolphins, a normally oceanic species, nosing their way around the entrance to a small river. If these normally deep-water animals can safely venture into a narrow channel, then why don't dolphins exploit the rich resources of the River Thames in England, the Mississippi in the USA, the Egyptian Nile or any others for that matter? Perhaps it is the need for a year-round food supply or variety of fish that is required; we don't know. But for whichever reason, the presence of dolphins in so few rivers highlights just how special these habitats must be and likewise just how sensitive the needs of the dolphins are.

Interactions with Man

Living inland, river dolphins have inevitably come into intimate contact with people and their activities. They feature in local culture and stories, ranging from the benign to the bizarre. The boto, for example, appears in many South American legends. In some, the dolphins take the form of men and seduce unmarried girls with irresistible charm, whilst in others they become lovely girls and lead young men into the water. Other stories imbue the dolphins with the souls of drowned people and secret cities of their own. River dolphins seem to have a certain magic even in areas where they are an everyday sight. In

Nepalese rivers, susu are still watched by villagers and fishermen with the same excitement and interest as they would be by tourists. At ferry crossings adults exclaim when they see a dolphin chasing fish flushed by the boat, while girls fishing in the shallows run laughing when a susu splashes them when chasing after the same prey.

Relationships can merge even more closely. Like coastal bottlenose dolphins, some Irrawaddy dolphins in Burma have struck up a cooperative relationship with local fishermen. Elsewhere, river dolphins are seen as a sign of abundant fish by searching fishermen and are looked upon favorably. River dolphins, however, are also exploited. In many areas it is believed that their organs have medicinal and aphrodisiac properties and so dolphins are sometimes caught. Fortunately, the financial reward for collecting these organs is too low to warrant intentionally capturing the dolphins. Fishermen more commonly catch them in nets, either on purpose or by accident, and eat their flesh or pour their oil back into the river to attract fish.

However, these deliberate catches have a comparatively minor impact in comparison with the huge and devastating changes that are occurring to the rivers in which the dolphins live, changes that are so major and so widespread that they threaten to completely eradicate the baiji, susu and bhulan in the imminent future.

The Yangtze, Ganges, Brahmaputra, Meghna, and Indus rivers in China, India, Nepal, Bangladesh and Pakistan are all central to the lives and economies of the people living beside them. They provide food, energy, drinking and bathing water, a means of transportation and waste disposal, and during floods they bathe the surrounding land in a fertile layer of silt. In fact these rivers provide such a wealth of resources to these poverty-stricken countries that huge demands are placed on them and progressively the characteristics of the rivers are being changed.

The abundant fish that support the dolphins also provide food and income for the local people. In the fishing process, however, dolphins are easily caught, asphyxiated or mutilated. One particularly gruesome method used in the Yangtze River to catch bottom-dwelling fish like catfish is known as the 'rolling hooks'. This method involves long fishing lines which are punctuated regularly by large hooks and despite being illegal this method may account for about half of the known baiji deaths. A less visible threat, but possibly just as important, comes from removing the fish: with fewer available, the dolphins face starvation, increased disease, or eviction from suitable areas.

Another form of environmental disturbance stems from the wide scale deforestation that has occurred on the land. As a result people have switched to collecting floating wood from the rivers for firewood and building materials. But in so doing, the piles of wood that make the refuges and nursery areas for fish no longer accumulate and key foraging areas for the dolphins are destroyed. With the deforestation has also come pollution, both in terms of direct chemical discharges and also as noise. We often overlook the impact of noise, but to animals dependent on this sense it can have a dramatic impact and even seemingly trivial noises may have major effects. For example, in the Karnali River in Nepal, the susu abandon their favored areas when the grass is harvested on the river banks. If cutting blades of grass can do this to the dolphins, one has to wonder about the effects of felling trees.

Another source of noise comes from boats. A favored dolphin habitat is where rivers meet and eddies and slack water are created. But these places are also favored for boat traffic, especially ferry crossings. Ferries were traditionally rowed or pulled by ropes and so made little if any noise other than that of people's voices and clumping of feet, but increasingly they are being motorized and so again threaten to force away the dolphins. As motor boats become more common and start to crowd the water, swimming away becomes futile and dolphins

Living in South American and Asian rivers brings the river dolphins into intimate contact with some of the most densely populated areas in the world. In many parts, the dolphins are respected by local people and figure heavily in folklore. Around the Amazon and Orinoco, for example, the boto is thought able to take on human form and walk amongst the townsfolk, and to help spirit healers cure people's illnesses. In Bangladesh, India, Nepal and Pakistan, the dolphins help guide fishermen to the best spots and sometimes even herd fish towards the boats.

The waterways in which the river dolphins evolved are being radically changed by the human populations that live around them. Over-fishing has reduced the dolphins' sources of food and the nets drown animals that blunder into them. Agricultural, domestic and industrial activities pollute the water, whilst damming, irrigation and water extraction alter annual floods and block off the dolphins' migration routes. Powerboats produce noise disturbance and direct collisions cause hideous injuries. In many areas the changes to the river dolphins' homes are so severe that many populations are now under direct threat of extinction.

simply have to bear the din. But becoming used to this also increases the danger of collisions, and many river dolphins are killed or horribly maimed by boat propellers.

A feature that makes the great rivers in which the dolphins live so productive is their propensity to flood. In doing so, they enrich the surrounding land, making it ideal for farming. Consequently it becomes densely populated. But as people settle, these same life-giving floods turn to life-threatening disasters, big enough to bring reporters scurrying from all over the world. Understandably, efforts are then made to control the river. Embankments are built to contain it, the sides are straightened and obstructions removed to speed flood water quickly away; the river then takes on the nature of a drain-pipe. The intricate patchwork of habitats – the sand bars, debris islands, eddies, loops and deep pools, that are home to the dolphins – is lost. The land, too, gradually becomes infertile as its nutrients are no longer replenished.

Another method of controlling the water's flow is to build high dams. These provide benefits by eliminating flooding, preventing water shortages, removing silt from water downstream to make it more suitable for drinking, and generating large amounts of cheap renewable power. These immediate and tangible benefits are popular with politicians who stake their personal reputations on them and push for huge impressive structures. Being big they are then designed by aspiring planners and engineers whose training and outlook makes them favor challenging designs to prove the worthiness of their involvement. Becoming sources of national pride, they also appeal to aid agencies and big business alike. Mega-projects are born. But having invested their personal reputations in dams, politicians are then compelled to have the work proceed despite the human and environmental costs and it is now clear that many high dams have destroyed the character of the rivers that they are supposed to regulate.

By putting an enormous wall across a river, the water behind it backs up and slows down, forming a lake. In it, the turbulence is lost and suspended sediment and debris are dropped. The water that flows out, freed of its sediment burden, then erodes the land further down and provides few nutrients for fish or agricultural land. The dams also hold back the floods and stop the areas around the rivers from being inundated. These rapid floods are essential in the life cycles of many fish species and, with their removal, food webs collapse. Migratory fish are also affected because the dams provide impenetrable obstacles and exclude them from traditional breeding sites. The dolphins are trapped in just the same way. The stagnant lakes behind the dams provide little sustenance whilst the wall itself divides and isolates populations like sheep in pens.

Other types of artificial barriers are the smaller-scale walls called barrages. These are gated so that during the floods they are left open to allow the huge flow to pass without causing damage, but as the flood recedes they are progressively closed to divert the water into irrigation and navigation canals. So, the gates potentially allow dolphins to travel up and down past them at certain times of year, but because the time at which they are open is during the flood, it may in fact be extremely difficult for the dolphins to swim upstream through them and so they act as one-way doors. These barrages are particularly common in Pakistan and today the six or seven hundred bhulan in existence are split into four or five artificially-isolated populations. As such these dolphins have become even more vulnerable to inbreeding and each group could easily be wiped out by a localized pollution incident or disease outbreak.

But there are ways to construct dams and barrages that cause less harm to dolphins and other natural wildlife. Multiple smaller dams near the top of rivers will have less impact than a single huge dam lower down. Where there is a choice, these walls could be constructed in tributaries where dolphins are naturally absent due to waterfalls or shallows. The use of fish-ladders to allow migrating fish, particularly salmon, to pass by otherwise impenetrable walls is now a routine part of dam making in many countries. It is surprising therefore, that this simple and comparatively cheap method has not been applied to let dolphins pass such deadly obstructions. Perhaps it is the minor economic value of river dolphins in the eyes of politicians and planners that has kept them low on the priority list.

However, solutions such as the construction of ladders, like the dams themselves, are never as simple as they seem. For a start, the behavior of dolphins around obstructions is poorly understood and it is not known if dolphins will actually use a ladder. Even worse, it is conceivable that the dolphins might only use them in one direction and so dams or barriers and their associated ladders would actually drain suitable habitats of dolphins in much the same way as a lobster pot is used to remove lobsters from the sea. Furthermore, by making dams and barriers more acceptable to conservationists concerned about dolphins, these gadgets will do nothing for the wider environment and take the most physically and politically visible but probably ecologically trivial species out of the argument, thus weakening the overall campaign against their construction.

Oil and gas have recently added another threat to the river dolphins' list. Gas fields lie locked below the Indus river in Pakistan. With the whole area being flooded each year, extracting it is an engineering challenge. To counter these problems a wall 16 miles (24 km) long has been constructed to divert the river away from one of the best remaining habitats for the bhulan. Altering the river's course, once again, will do little to help the dolphins.

Each of the individual threats that face the river dolphins is grim, but put together they make an overwhelmingly depressing picture. Of all the stories, that of the Chinese baiji is the worst. With pollution, dam construction, river simplification, dredging, boat disturbance, over-fishing, entanglement, land-reclamation and propeller strikes, their populations have sunk to piteously low levels. It is currently the rarest dolphin in the world, with probably fewer than 150 left alive today. To picture this number, imagine walking down the aisle of an underground train. If the seats were filled by baijis rather than people, you would have met every single one in existence by the time you got halfway down the train. To add a further insult, the latest mega-project, due to be completed in 2009, the Three Gorges high dam, will degrade another 10% of their remaining habitat. This is clearly the eleventh hour for the baiji.

In response, the Chinese government has attempted to promote wider support for their conservation by giving them first-order legal protection, designating them as a National Treasure of China, has backed research, issued stamps showing the baiji and even promoted baiji beer. But the demands of the human population for water, food and energy provide an urgency that easily overrides consideration for the natural fauna.

In view of this critical situation, there have been moves to develop a captive breeding colony and semi-natural reserve until some of their real habitat can be restored. But, such action requires a difficult decision: should the last wild baijis be caught to stock the experimental reserve? This might be the most efficient way of saving the species, but given their equivocal record in captivity, many consider this too big a gamble. Furthermore, if these animals were removed, what incentive would there be to restore the ecology of their natural home? Without the dolphins as an emblem to be proud of, what hope would there be for the other plants and animals of the Yangtze?

Facing extinction: of all the world's dolphin species, the baiji is the most threatened. There are probably fewer than 150 left alive today and these few face a depressing list of dangers. As a result, there have been attempts to set up a captive breeding colony and semi-natural reserve until their real habitat can be restored. But the demands of the human population living along the banks of the Yangtze make true .restoration of the river seem very unlikely. For these dolphins, the future looks very bleak indeed.

Dolphins strand for a variety of reasons. Ill or injured animals may try and rest in shallow waters and be left high and dry by the tide, dead animals may be washed or blown ashore, others may become disorientated in coastal waters. Whatever the reason, strandings are surprisingly frequent and occur on most beaches from time to time.

Strandings

Perhaps the closest encounter that many of us have with a wild dolphin is upon finding one stranded on the beach, and much of what we know about dolphins comes from these arrivals. Single strandings of dead or dying whales and dolphins are common and we should expect nothing less based on their abundance at sea, but strandings of groups of seemingly healthy animals are harder to explain. Like many unsolved mysteries, including the dinosaur extinctions or the construction of Stonehenge, scientists and non-scientists alike indulge in the wildest flights of fancy when it comes to explaining mass strandings. Suggested reasons include inner ear parasite infestations, mass suicide, noise disturbance from military testing, unwell school leaders, misdirected magnetic navigation, confusion in shallow water and earthquakes. Whilst some of these are nonsensical, others have nuggets of evidence in their favor, but the jury is still out as to why they occur. What is certain, is that these events do happen every year. In most years, for example, sperm whales strand on the North Sea coastline. Although single live animals become beached, they as frequently occur in groups. Sometimes whales will spend days or weeks in shallow bays or estuaries from which they may be coaxed with boats into deeper water. Once out they may never be seen again or simply turn around and swim back to the shallows to become trapped by the next receding tide. Once stranded, their fates are sealed. Without supporting water, their huge weight crushes their own internal organs and without a cooling water jacket they quickly cook in their own body heat. The reasons for these annual European events are a subject of much debate. The sperm whales that strand are always males and strandings usually occur between November and February. It has been suggested, therefore, that these seasonal events may be linked to the southward migrations of the normally Arctic-living males, to join up with the females living in the tropics. As the North Sea has a large entrance in the north, whales moving south could enter it thinking that they were still in the open sea and then become gradually more and more confined and confused and eventually miss the shallow southern exit, the English Channel. The 'North Sea sperm whale trap' hypothesis is an attractive idea but unfortunately does not explain why whales also strand in just the same way on coasts bordering the open ocean elsewhere! Other annual stranding events have a more obvious cause. Each spring on the coasts of southern England dozens of common dolphins wash up dead or dying. Many have tell-tale signs of interactions with fishing nets. Some have cuts from nets, others have had their fins and flukes cut off, whilst others still carry pieces of net wrapped around their bodies.

Strandings occur on almost every beach at some time or other and if you are on one, there is a chance that you will come across a stranded dolphin or whale or even a mass stranding. If so, the first thing to do will be to find out whether the animal(s) is alive or dead. If you are unsure then watch and listen for breathing through the blowhole on the top of the head. Many of the deep diving cetaceans can hold their breath for long periods, so if you are unsure wait a little longer. While waiting, keep your distance: a distressed animal may thrash around and injure bystanders. If it is definitely dead, then try and work out which species it is, note any distinctive features, estimate its length, if possible take notes and photographs and remember the spot where it is. Strandings schemes, which collect and carry out post-mortem examinations of marine mammals, operate around many coastlines, so contact them as soon as possible. Don't assume that someone else will — it is astonishing what people walk past without thinking to tell any-body. If the animal is likely to get washed away, then tie it to something at the top of the beach; discarded rope is a universal component of any strand-line. Finally, as with any rotting body, take hygiene precautions. Try to avoid touching it, wash your hands as soon as possible if you have, and keep children and dogs away. And beware, large rotting whales produce copious quantities of gas and do explode!

If the animal(s) is alive, then swift action is required if it is to be rescued or if its suffering is to be minimized. The first thing to do is to get appropriate help. A strandings scheme, if there is one, should be the first to call. If there isn't, then call the police, local authority, veterinary surgeon, marine park or animal welfare organization. While waiting for help, douse the animal(s) with sea water to keep it cool and prevent its skin from drying out, but also take care not to allow water to enter its blowhole or it will drown. If you have to move the animal, do so on a tar-paulin, and never drag it over the ground or pull it by the flukes, flippers or dorsal fin. Keep yourself clear of the mouth and tail for your own sake and avoid breathing your germs over it or scaring it by talking loudly. Ask onlookers to stay at a safe distance, but co-opt anybody if you need them. When help does arrive, don't be too hopeful; the best decision may well be to put the animal down. Finally, if it is to be re-floated, remember your own safety as well: life-jackets, waterproofs, wet suits and a life-guard are all good measures to avoid further casualties.

Some rescues of live stranded cetaceans take only minutes and involve just a few people but others, particularly for bigger species and mass strandings, require huge efforts. Teams of people, earth-moving machinery, specialized flotation equip-ment, veterinary expertise, boats and helicopters may all be involved. However, the motivation that people have to carry out these labors is often very different. Many rescuers focus on animal welfare and aim purely to relieve the animals of their

suffering and accept that the euthanasia of injured or sick animals is just as valid an outcome as putting more healthy ones back into the sea. Other people feel that crowd control is most important and that the animals should be left alone to die with dignity. Others feel that all animals should be put back into the water at all costs. Many, motivated by conservation concerns, feel that the efforts and resources would be better spent stop-ping the human activities that may lead to cetaceans becoming disorientated, injured or sick rather than focusing on the small proportion that wash ashore while still alive. To confuse the debate still further, surprisingly few animals have been followed with electronic tags or natural marks after they have been 'rescued' and so the success and therefore value of these attempts is, in most cases, unknown.

In contrast the carcasses of dolphins often provide important information, not only about why they might have stranded or been ill in the first place but also about their general biology, diet, growth and so on. They also indicate how humans have affected their lives. As we have seen, strandings of asphyxiated dolphins may indicate the occurrence of fisheries interactions further off-shore, and pollutants in their tissues have proved a link between our pollution and their disease. When live stranded animals are followed after a rescue they can provide useful insights. For example, an oceanic bottlenose dolphin which stranded and was subsequently treated, was recently released from Florida wearing a satellite transmitter. Although it moved widely after release, it stayed within waters of a precise temper-ature, even to the point that it changed its movements when weather fronts passed over the sea. In doing so, this one animal put into question some of our existing ideas about the structure of populations of bottlenose dolphins living in the Atlantic and also gave us new clues about how dolphins choose their routes across oceans. Most strandings are found by chance, so if you are going out for a walk on the beach, keep your eyes peeled!

Wherever substantial fishing effort with nets and marine mammals coincide, entanglement occurs and this currently poses the greatest threat to many dolphin populations. In New Zealand the numbers of Hector's dolphins caught in coastal gillnets were so high that a marine mammal sanctuary was set up specifically to protect these vulnerable animals.

Dolphin Research

To sustainably conserve, manage or exploit dolphins, we need good information on them, particularly with regard to their distribution, numbers, interactions with other species and their underlying biology. But for researchers, gathering this information is far from simple. Dolphins are wide-ranging mammals; where they are one day is no guarantee of where they will be the next. Some populations may never come near land and others are so shy that they are rarely seen at all. All species spend only a fraction of their time at the surface and carry out most of their activities out of sight. Neither do dolphins leave signs of their passing; they don't dig burrows, nor leave droppings or tracks. It can be no surprise, then, that we know far less about them than we do about most land mammals and there are certainly many populations that have yet to be discovered.

The information that is being gathered about dolphins is increasing at a fantastic rate, particularly in the last three decades. This is partly due to the growth of public and scientific interest in dolphins but also from the invention of some highly powerful research tools.

One of the major leaps in dolphin science came when dolphins were captured and maintained in captivity. By just trying to keep the animals alive and healthy, much was learnt about their biology, illnesses and dietary requirements. With captive breeding programs, data have been gained on their reproductive biology, their behavior towards calves, breeding rates and so on. Studies on their behavior quickly showed that dolphins are far more intelligent than most other mammals and that they are equipped with some fantastic skills like echolocation. This new information has changed the general perception of dolphins. In the eyes of many, they are no longer simply the warm-blooded equivalents of fish, but intelligent, charismatic and vulnerable creatures. Ironically, this new viewpoint has led to an intolerance towards holding dolphins captive, and in some countries facilities have been forced to shut down, while in others higher standards have been demanded.

Despite the undoubted value of studying captive animals, many aspects of dolphin life can only be discovered by looking at their activities in the wild. There is no way, for example, that the patterns of social behavior observed in aquaria are representative of what actually occurs at sea. But studying wild dolphins is far from simple. Observers out on the water are at the mercy of the weather and dependent on expensive boats and aircraft. Recently, the evolution of some ingenious techniques has made this work far easier. One of these has been the development of individual identification. As a principle it was used as far back as ancient Greece, where fishermen who accidentally captured dolphins cut small notches into their dorsal fins so that they could be recognised again. In more recent times, a variety of tags and markers were put on dolphins for the same purpose. But in the 1970s a revolution occurred. It was discovered that individual dolphins of many species possess sufficient natural markings that they can be individually identified from photographs, and 'photo-identification' (or photo-ID) was born. Now researchers can go out to sea, photograph the backs and dorsal fins of the dolphins that they see and later match the individuals with photographs from previous trips. Marks such as tatters in the dorsal fin, scratch marks or tiny differences in the coloration patterns of individuals have proved most effective. With this simple approach, encounters with wild dolphins have changed from perplexing glimpses of anonymous animals to in-depth views of the movements of particular individuals, the patterns of association between them and even the progress of diseases through wild populations. Photo-ID also provides a way to estimate the number of animals in a population using a simple mathematical method called mark-recapture.

But despite photo-ID being a powerful tool, now applied world-wide to more than half of the dolphin species, it cannot be used to study dolphins in inaccessible areas, for shy species, or for populations with thousands of individuals. Instead, other methods must be applied. An alternative approach to estimate how many animals are in a population is to use a procedure called line-transect surveying. This involves criss-crossing a piece of water in a ship or plane, counting the animals seen and recording their distance and angle from the vessel's path. From the number counted and the area of water scanned, the density of dolphins can be calculated and if the range of a population is known, the total population size can be estimated.

Similar surveys have also been designed, but instead of observers looking for dolphins, the calls the dolphins make underwater are recorded. Although these techniques are still in their infancy, listening to the vocalizations of dolphins has already proved effective in studies of their feeding behavior and modes of communication. To track the movements of wild dolphins and other marine mammals a variety of high-tech transmitters and data loggers have been built. The most simple are transmitters which continuously send out a beeping radio signal. An animal fitted with such a transmitter can then be followed by boat or plane wherever it goes. But following animals for long periods is expensive so transmitters have been built that send their signals directly to satellites and then back to earth. As micro-technology has become more sophisticated, electronic tags have been built that are sensitive to their surroundings and transmit this information in the signals to the satellites. So not only can a researcher know where a dolphin tagged the month before now is, but he or she can also find out how deep and how long it is diving, and how fast it is swimming.

Although these transmitters are wondrous devices, their attachment has always been a problem because dolphin skin is smooth and most dolphins lack a neck around which to fasten a collar. Instead, transmitters are usually attached to the dorsal fin by one or more bolts made from surgical plastic. As well as causing minor injury, these systems require that the animal be handled. Catching wild dolphins always involves a degree of stress for the animals but perhaps more importantly, if it is a wide-ranging species, it may well lose touch with its school-mates whilst the tagging is carried out. The resulting data may therefore record the wanderings of a dolphin that has lost its compatriots rather than any normal behavior. Recent developments, however, may have got round this problem. A radio transmitter and data recorder package can be fixed to a big rubber sucker and the package stuck to the dolphin as it passes a boat. This arrangement may only stay on for a few hours but it offers the possibility of answering dozens of unsolved questions.

Dolphins can also be watched from shore and much has been learnt about their behavior in coastal waters and rivers with this simple approach. Such watches can be enhanced if a surveyor's theodolite is used. These tripod-mounted devices work like gun-sights and are used to precisely measure angles. When pointed at groups of dolphins surfacing at sea, theodolites can be used to calculate their position accurately and when combined with a stop watch or video camera, their swimming speeds, length of dives and the spacings between individuals can be determined. Because observers working from a cliff top are unlikely to influence the behavior of the animals that they are watching, these techniques are ideal for studying how dolphins behave with and without other types of disturbance. The route they choose over a particular area, the effects of boat traffic, human swimmers, underwater noise and dredging activities have all been studied in this way.

Most of what we know about dolphin anatomy, diseases and

In the mid 1970s a revolution occurred when it was discovered that individual dolphins in wild populations could be distinguished from one another using photographs of the scars and blemishes on their dorsal fins and backs. 'Photo-identification' was born. Since then this powerful and non-invasive technique has been extended to study the ecology of at least half of the world's dolphin species and has given powerful insights into their movement patterns, social systems, life expectancies and reproductive rates.

The combination of original thinking and new technologies has begun to answer some
age-old questions about the lives of dolphins. Studies of the properties of plankton at night and new
camera technology, for example, may crack the mystery of how dolphins swim with such efficiency.

the effects of pollution comes from animals that have washed ashore after dying at sea. Strandings occur along almost every coast and their distribution can sometimes be used to work out where a particular species lives. Furthermore, the timing of strandings may also indicate the occurrence of unusual events. For example, sudden strandings of animals with full stomachs and net marks might indicate an interaction with human fisheries, whilst live strandings of emaciated or feeble animals might indicate a disease outbreak or a poisoning event.

Stranded animals have also given us most of our information on dolphin body sizes and color patterns. Much of the information in the 'Dolphin Facts' section of this book comes from these sources. Furthermore, their internal anatomy can give us information not only on the specializations among dolphins but, when compared between species, about their behavior. For example, almost nothing is known about the patterns of mating in most dolphins. But comparative studies of testis size have shown that male common dolphins have testes that are proportionally four times the size of those in bottlenose and humpback dolphins. Information gleaned from similar studies on birds and other mammals would suggest that male common dolphins are less able to exclude other males from a female than bottlenose or humpback dolphins and so they have evolved a strategy of producing large quantities of sperm to ensure that they, rather than other males, are the ones that father a female's offspring.

The actual practicalities of gaining information from stranded carcasses, however, is often the least pleasant of all marine mammal work. Animals may sometimes strand after many weeks decaying at sea and often their smell will indicate their presence before they come into sight. Nevertheless, even a rotten carcass can be useful. The skeleton may be complete and with it, the identification of its species and some information about its past life; the teeth can be used to age it and remains in the stomach indicate what the animal ate just before it died. Fresher carcasses provide information about the factors that cause death in these species, the diseases and parasites that they carry and the burdens of pollutants in their tissues. The presence of fetuses in females may indicate at what age they start to give birth and in what season breeding may occur. Increasingly, samples are also being used to find out about the genetic composition within populations and the use of proteins and fats in dolphin tissues may give more indications about their long-term dietary habits. Tissue samples can also be taken from living animals without the need to capture or handle them. A range of darts and scrapers have been developed to take tiny samples of skin and blubber from dolphins as they swim past a boat. Crossbows, dart-guns and poles have all been used to obtain these biopsy samples, which have later been analysed to examine the genetic make-up of individuals, work out what sex the animals are and look at the levels of pollutants in their tissues. By its very nature biopsy sampling is an emotive issue and while many people feel that stealing a piece of skin from a passing dolphin is unacceptable, others feel that the benefits of the information when properly analysed far outweigh any cost to the animal.

Perhaps one of the major thrills for researchers working on dolphins is the way in which a new but seemingly unremarkable observation can suddenly be turned to answer an important and previously intractable problem. How dolphins slip through the water with such efficiency has been one such enigma. Dolphins and whales swim with an effectiveness that is the envy of ship, submarine and torpedo designers the world over and many attempts have been made to find out how they do it. Their most obvious characteristic is their streamlined shape, but studies using rigid model dolphins have not proved them terribly efficient, so researchers have searched for other explanations. Many have been suggested over the years and have included the secretion of oil droplets, sloughing skin, tiny surface crinkles and the damping effects of the blubber layer. But to test the importance of these, the way in which water actually flows over the bodies of dolphins swimming at top speed needs to be understood. Such studies are routinely carried out for a wide range of other applications. New car designs, for example, are tested in wind tunnels where thin streams of smoke are moved around upwind of the car and the exact paths that they take are recorded. Any features that cause excessive turbulence or disruptions to the flow can then be redesigned. Insect and bird flight has also been studied in similar ways, while fish swimming has been investigated using streams of dye or air bubbles. But building tanks to study the patterns of fluid movement around dolphins swimming at their top speed is extremely difficult and the construction of such a tank would be nothing to building a chamber to test the flow around a charging whale. And this is where a simple observation linked with modern technology has provided a solution.

Ever since the first sailors took to the sea at night, people have been awe-struck by the fiery displays put on by bioluminescent plankton. Tiny organisms, which include bacteria and dinoflagellates, live suspended in the water and use special chemiluminescent reactions to produce flashes of green light when they are disturbed. On dark nights a ship moving across water rich in these organisms will generate an eerie glowing wake whilst the water crashing over the bows will produce spectacular bursts of light like exploding fireworks. Torpedoes and dolphins produce fiery trails too and many war-time mariners were given a heart-stopping moment when they saw the trails of dolphins racing towards their ships.

Returning to the quest to uncover the dolphins' swimming secrets, the luminous plankton provide a unique natural flow marker for anything moving through waters that they infest. Several previous attempts have been made to observe dolphins riding the bow waves of ships at night to glimpse the path of the water as it flows around their bodies, but the dolphins' movements are just too quick to be plain to the naked eye and the stream of light too faint to photograph or film. But new image-intensifying video technology, developed for entirely different purposes, has changed that and these events can now be recorded and watched over and over again in slow motion. Furthermore, because the plankton only begin to light up when they are placed under a particular level of disturbance, the pressure fields and types of flow around the animals can be measured. So the combination of an old observation and a new technology may indeed reveal the dolphin's secrets of efficient swimming.

In a similar fashion, video technology may offer us a chance to look over the shoulder of a free-swimming dolphin to see what it sees and so begin to better understand how it navigates and hunts. Video cameras can now be made sufficiently small that when fitted into waterproof housings and attached to the back of a seal or dolphin they don't significantly disrupt its natural behaviour. Seals have been the first to wear these new packages, as attaching them to their fur is relatively straightforward, and the films that the animals have brought back have been astonishing. We have been able to watch how they navigate over reefs and choose a spot to feed, where they hide when they see a large shark and how they tussle with smaller sharks over scraps of food. Like radio and satellite transmitters, attaching these packages to slippery dolphin skin is still a major problem but once solved we will be able to see what really goes on far below the waves.

In addition to those just outlined, many other techniques, borrowed from different branches of science or specifically formulated for dolphin research, are now available to further our knowledge of dolphins. But none of these tools is of any use unless they are fitted to a purpose. Unfortunately, for many researchers that purpose is now the urgent need to conserve the species or populations on which they work.

Tell tails: the appearance of every dolphin tells a story. These two Atlantic spotted dolphins may at first sight appear similar, but the trailing dolphin has injured its tail. The normal notch between its two tail flukes has been overshadowed by a larger one probably from a bite from another dolphin or a shark. Like tassels, parasitic barnacles also cling to the tails of both dolphins.

Dolphins, along with the whales, are the ultimate in conservation icons, but maintaining their populations is far harder than for equivalent mammals on land. They can range over thousands of miles, pay no attention to national boundaries, switch prey and behavior overnight and live lives as long as ours. Dolphin conservation is an enormous challenge.

Dolphin Conservation

We can now say with depressing certainty that every dolphin alive today is affected by human activities. Underwater noise masks their calls, overfishing changes their menu, and ubiquitous pollutants alter the cellular processes that help them reproduce and fight disease. Where our impacts have been most severe, populations and species have declined to the very edge of extinction, and with the world's human population growing, our pressures on the environment continue to intensify. More dolphins are now dying each year from entanglement in fishing nets than whales ever did at the height of the whaling era. And although the most damaging pollutants are now banned in many countries, old emissions continue to be passed up food chains and become concentrated in each new dolphin generation. Clearly, the status quo is unacceptable. So what can be done?

With dolphins being held in captivity, wide-ranging research and the production of popular television programs, the scientific and public appreciation of these animals has grown enormously. After all, which other creatures could make fifty newspaper reporters run out on to a tidal mudflat but a stranded group of whales or dolphins? In the minds of many, we see them as we would like to see ourselves. They represent free spirits, beauty, friendliness and marvels of design. And with the admiration that follows knowledge, comes concern. Like the whales, dolphins elicit a strong urge to conserve the environment. Environmental organizations that sport dolphins in their logos or in campaigns gain greater attention than those that support other species. For many they are the ambassadors for the seas and great rivers.

The public and scientific demand for action has forced governments and international organizations to respond, but protecting dolphins, or any marine organism, is far more complicated than conserving equivalent species on land. Marine ecosystems are more intricate than most terrestrial ones, as managers of fishery policy have found to our cost. Being harder to understand, the appropriate levels of exploitation and remedial action are never as clear. We traditionally manage resources by imposing limits on our exploitation, usually in the form of boundaries like reserves, wildlife havens and national borders, but these are only useful for species that have the most limited ranges. Consequently, management tends to focus on regulating impacts through the designation of quotas for exploitation or disturbance. For example, the Inter-American Tropical Tuna Commission set limits on the number of dolphins killed during tuna-fishing operations in the Eastern Tropical Pacific. When a tuna boat reached its limit, it was to switch to an alternative fishing method. By forcing us to quantify and limit our impacts, the quota approach has the potential to be highly successful, but it has two important weaknesses.

Firstly, it is no good if one country behaves in a responsible manner when another that shares the same resource does not, because in a free market, the country with the cheapest exploitation can usually undercut the others. This principle is known as the 'Tragedy of the commons' and is most commonly illustrated with an example from farming in the Middle Ages. Whilst villagers managed their own lands with restraint, they didn't on the common land used by all. If a villager grazed an extra sheep on the commons, the advantage was all on his side, while the over-grazing problem was shared by the whole village. The only way that the neighbors could make up for it was by bringing in extra sheep of their own, and so the pastures were soon ruined. The aquatic resources are our commons today and the 'Tragedy' stays with us as the history of whaling admirably demonstrates. Furthermore, market forces may even favor over-exploitation. Unfortunately, it often makes better financial sense to completely mine-out a resource then let regeneration keep pace with a smaller harvest, for when the resource has been exhausted, the resulting revenue can be turned to exploiting something else.

But market forces need not always rule; whaling, for example, is now only a fraction of the reckless exploitation that it once was. Co-ordinated multi-state regulation, in the form of the International Whaling Commission, has constrained this abuse and offered a long-term future for the industry. For dolphins, however, there is no such Commission and the range of problems that they face is considerably more diverse. Current protection comes under local, national and international legislation which varies widely in remit and efficiency. The Marine Mammal Protection Act (1972) in the United States is amongst the most stringent, with heavy penalties for infringement, and it also has a remit to sponsor research. In Europe, protection comes under a variety of agreements overseen by European law. In many other countries, particularly in the developing world, few laws exist, and where they do, finances to enforce them are often lacking. Considerable progress, however, is being made by bodies such as the IUCN Cetacean Specialist Group, which identifies problem areas, particularly in underdeveloped nations, and facilitates action to address them. Furthermore, conservation bodies, like the Whale and Dolphin Conservation Society and the Cetacean Society International, are doing much to highlight the plight of endangered dolphins and use money from public donations to fund research, education and campaigning.

The second weakness of the quota approach arises when there is insufficient biological information, whether on the species involved, the nature of the problem or a workable solution. Even when there is sufficient political will, gaining this information is much more difficult than it is for terrestrial animals. With our latest scientific tools, a research team cannot answer the questions needed to construct effective conservation strategies in a month or a year. A population that is changing in size for the better or worse, for example, might only show this change after a decade or more of research. But, for many highly threatened species or populations, a delay as long as this could easily take them past the point of recovery. And, in many cases, the links between human activities and harm may never be demonstrable. Furthermore, the picture can become even more complicated by the behavior of the dolphins themselves. Being predators they are dependent on the availability of their prey. However, little in the sea is constant and so every dolphin species has had to evolve to be sufficiently adaptable to be able to switch to another source of prey or simply go through a fasting period if their current food supply disappears. Similarly, if dolphins are prevented for some reason from feeding in a particular fashion they will quickly replace it with another. As a consequence dolphins and most other marine mammals don't exhibit the impacts of changes in their environment and instead often manifest them in subtle and sometimes totally unexpected ways. Hawaiian monk seals have provided an extreme example. Usually the number of females is considered as the critical component of an endangered population and that as long as there are enough males to mate with these females, the number of males and juveniles are relatively unimportant. However, these seals, which live around the islands of Hawaii and nowhere else, have experienced large declines in their populations and in the process the sex ratio has become skewed so that there are slightly more males than females. The seals mate on land and in the mating process the males nip at the backs of the females. With too many males,

Even if a dolphin population is in trouble, the individuals you find at sea will rarely show any visible signs of it.

competition between them is intense and the females often sustain many bites when gangs of males fight over each female. After mating, the females usually go back to the sea to feed but they leave a bloody trail in the water and many of them either don't ever come back or return with huge and often fatal shark bites. So in the following year, there are even fewer females and the males fight even more intensely. Few people would have predicted that once reduced to only a few individuals, the future of such a vulnerable population would be jeopardized by the behaviour of its own individuals. Clearly, whilst scientific research may be able to guide a debate and supply valuable insights, it can rarely provide the answers. Instead, managers are often forced to deal with uncertainty and have to make informed best guesses about the allowable number of animals that can be killed or disturbed.

One solution to this problem has been called the precautionary principle, which asserts that if an action's impact is unknown, it should be prohibited until it is proved not to harm the species of interest. This attractive approach, when applied to a problem, often does much to unravel the issues but rarely solves it. The oil industry provides a current example. In order to find oil or gas below the seabed, seismic surveys are carried out. In these, a ship zigzags across the sea towing airguns and hydrophones. The airguns make loud bangs which travel through the water and rocks below. The returning echoes are received by the hydrophones and the data used to identify suitable rock formations. Seismic surveying is really just echolocation on an enormous scale. However, there are many concerns that the volume and frequencies of the bangs could disturb, deafen or kill marine mammals in the vicinity. The potential is clear but the magnitude of impact, whether minor or major, is far harder to prove. If the precautionary principle were strictly applied, then no seismic surveys could go ahead until there is more information. However, the impacts may never be understood and

meanwhile the demand for oil continues. Withholding permission to explore would mean a huge loss of revenue and jobs for any country, and exploration would be taken up elsewhere anyway. In consequence, seismic surveys currently take place throughout continental shelf waters all over the world. In some areas, like in British waters, a middle road has been taken; airguns are used as little as possible, observers are put on boats to look out for marine mammals and the volume produced by the guns is gradually increased before a survey begins, giving animals a chance to escape. But nobody knows whether these measures actually make any difference to the marine mammals that are living in the areas that are subjected to the seismic surveys.

Much of the reason that these surveys go ahead, despite the uncertainty, stems from the political power wielded by industry. But focused pressure from the public and media can be just as strong. In the 1970s huge pressure from the American public and scientists forced the Government to introduce the Marine Mammal Protection Act which drastically reduced dolphin kills made by the tuna-fishing industry, whilst in the 1990s, campaigning by Greenpeace and pressure from the European public reversed a decision by the British Government and Shell to dump the Brent Spar oil platform at sea. Without people expressing their distaste neither of these landmark events would have occurred, but still hundreds of issues remain unsung and apathy on the part of the public may well prove the dolphins' greatest enemy.

In the last thirty years, we have come a long way in our devotion to, understanding and conservation of dolphins. How we proceed in the next thirty will be critical for the wellbeing of the most endangered populations and species. But whatever happens, conservation is not a task that can be finished; the actions required to save dolphins will need to continue for as long as we disturb, exploit, plough, ply and pollute their habitats. Dolphin conservation, as an issue, will never go away.

A celebrity. 'Kess', an adult female bottlenose dolphin, lived off the coast of north-east Scotland and spent much of her time in a narrow channel running between two villages. Her crooked spine and leaning dorsal fin made her easily recognizable whilst her antics and those of her calves gave pleasure and inspiration to many who saw her.

Getting to Know a Wild Dolphin

Throughout this book the value of being able to identify individual dolphins in wild populations has arisen over and over again. Our knowledge of their seasonal and daily movements, patterns of association, longevity of bonds and so on have been strengthened by our ability to recognize one from another. In the early days of dolphin research, animals were followed with radio transmitters or recognized by man-made marks on their dorsal fins. But with sufficient care and attention, individuals can be distinguished from one another and followed through time by natural features alone.

I first began working with a research group in northern Scotland on a resident population of bottlenose dolphins. Our efforts were focused on going out into the local waters for day-long boat trips and photographing the animals we came across. Later, in a darkened room, we would pore over these photographs and distinguish one dolphin from another by their natural marks and give each a unique number and a memory-jogging name, based on one peculiarity or another. At the beginning, we had no idea how many dolphins there were in the population, but a decade later, we now know almost exactly how many individuals there are, which areas they favor and how these change with season, how diseases affect different age groups and what social patterns they have adopted. As time and surveys go on, this data-base will begin to answer many more questions about whether the population's size is stable, how long Scottish bottlenose dolphins live, how many of their calves survive and perhaps one day, why they have chosen this part of the North Sea in which to live rather than any other.

Of the 130 individuals in the population, one animal, an adult female called Kess, stood out from the rest. Her distinctive features and regular sightings made her the most popular dolphin with our research group. She was instantly recognizable from a distance due to an unusual distortion of her spine which gave her body a kinked appearance between the dorsal fin and tail. Her dorsal fin was unusually broad, bent over to the right and had three tiny nicks in its trailing edge. Her skin was the color of other adult bottlenose dolphins in the area, a rich chocolatey brown with a hint of grey. In places it was criss-crossed with the pale scars from other dolphins' teeth. Kess's swimming was distinctly slower than other adult dolphins, probably as a result of her deformity, but she was capable of turns of speed and could leap clear of the water when the occasion took her.

Kess did not live on her own but was very much part of the wider dolphin community. We would usually find her in groups of three or four animals and, like most other dolphins in the population, she notched up many companions in the course of a year. But these acquaintances were not random and took on a complex hierarchy. Most constant were her own calves and then came one or more adult females.

The large sheltered estuarine area in which these Scottish dolphins live is called the Moray Firth which is shaped like a wedge and has its apex pointing south-west towards the heart of the Scottish mainland. Early on in our studies, we found that the dolphins use different parts of the Moray Firth during the seasons. They tend to be found farther out into the open sea during the winter and deeper into the estuary during the summer. Throughout these seasonal movements, Kess was always in the group of dolphins nearest the head of the estuary in the south-west, in the most sheltered waters. These seasonal inshore movements regularly took her to a narrow inlet called the Kessock Channel, after which she was named.

Kess had four calves in the eight years that we were able to record the events in her life. We saw her first in 1990 and she was accompanied by a calf that appeared to be about two years old. Named 'Frith' after one of our research team, this young dolphin showed an obsession with boats and would race over to them, rolling upside-down and skimming along under the water just inches in front of their bows. This habit allowed us to glimpse his belly and see that he was a male. Several times that summer Kess and Frith were joined by a larger juvenile male called 'Vampire Victim' after two little circular bite marks behind his dorsal fin. By his size we judged him to have been around four or five years old. In subsequent years, we often saw him with Kess and wondered whether he was one of Kess's earlier calves. In the autumn of 1990 we came across Kess and Frith in the channel but now Kess was also accompanied by a tiny calf. 'Wee Frith' was seen with Kess several times over that winter but the following spring it looked extremely thin with the outline of its ribs being clearly visible. The next time we were able to find Kess and Frith they showed no interest in boats and the tiny calf was gone.

Less than a year later, Kess was accompanied by a new calf, 'Frithlet'. All appeared well with this youngster until the summer of 1993 when people began to report seeing a dolphin entangled in fishing net thrashing about at the surface. On investigation the dolphin was the year-old calf, Frithlet, but there was nothing attached to its tail. Instead it had developed a humped back not dissimilar to Kess's and seemed unable to bend its spine vertically, and so swam by sweeping its tail from side to side. Soon afterwards it was found dead on the shore of the Kessock Channel. A post-mortem examination showed that Frithlet was female and the deformity had distorted both her skeleton and muscles. The following summer, Kess gave birth to another calf, 'Kesslet' who like her living brother, Frith, spent hours energetically circling boats to the delight of fishermen, locals and tourists alike.

In the early spring of 1998, after eight years and many hundreds of encounters with Kess after she was first identified, we heard of an adult female bottlenose dolphin washed up on the beach. The remains were decomposed but a kinked spine was still clearly visible making it immediately clear that the carcass in front of us was that of Kess. A post-mortem examination showed that her stomach was empty and her fat reserves had been severely depleted in the period before her death. Her distorted back was the result of a lateral deviation of the spine with which she was probably born. As no other reasons why she should have died were apparent it seems likely that she probably couldn't catch enough food to survive in that final winter.

Whilst Frith and Kesslet still use their usual haunts, Kessock feels strangely empty without Kess the dolphin. It has been a privilege to get to know a little about the activities of a wild dolphin that chose to live in and around a tiny inlet fringed by peoples' houses, shops and schools. Kess taught us much about the biology of bottlenose dolphins. She showed us that wild dolphins with significant disabilities are capable of surviving and successfully raising young, that upon the loss of a calf a female dolphin will conceive a new one within months and perhaps even before losing a previous calf; that births occur during the summer and that calves, male and female, will stay in the areas in which they were raised even when their mother is no longer there. Kess may even provide the first piece needed to solve the puzzle of why the population uses the Moray Firth area at all. No other dolphins were ever found further inshore than Kess. Her deformity appeared to weaken her swimming, perhaps making her less able to ride out rough seas than other animals. Maybe then it is the sheltered waters of the Moray Firth and particularly its inner channels that makes this area so special for these dolphins. Seeing which dolphin chooses to move in to fill Kess's place will make or break this hypothesis. Only time and further research work will tell.

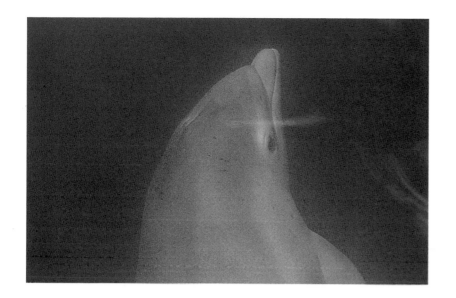

*Clockwise from top right: 'Frith' often takes great interest in boats. 'Frithlet', born in 1992, developed
a crooked back similar to her mother's. 'Vampire Victim' was often seen with Kess and her calves and may
have been their older brother. Like Frith, 'Kesslet' often approaches boats to ride their bow-wave.*

Watch how you watch. In many countries where dolphins are within easy reach of shore, dolphin-watching companies have started up. Boat tours are common and offer opportunities to see wild dolphins. But there are increasing concerns that dolphins may be disrupted by traffic whirring around above their heads. Engine noise can mask communication calls and interfere with echolocation, whilst collisions may be fatal. As a response, in many areas guidelines and rules for operators have been created. If you do go out, pick a licensed operator and if you feel that the boat is harassing the animals or if you think that you are too close, don't be afraid to say so.

Getting Involved

Dolphins are much more common than people think. Every ocean and most seas are home to one or more species. Furthermore, they are not necessarily somewhere over the horizon. Wild dolphins come close inshore and can often be seen from headlands, bridges, on ferry crossings and even from guesthouse windows! Where they are rare, local newspapers may report sightings but, ironically, where they are common few people mention them unless asked. With a little homework, patience and a keen eye it is not difficult to find and watch these inspiring creatures in the wild.

As a result of their widespread distribution, their appeal and an increase in people wanting to see them, dolphin-watching is now possible in coastal areas all over the world. Trips can be taken by land, air and sea. Land-based watching offers the most freedom. In many areas, you can sit for hours on a beach watching animals within only a few feet of you and without fear of disturbing them. What could be more beautiful than lying on a beach on a star-lit night listening to dolphins blowing nearby!

The majority of organized trips are boat-based and range from brief excursions lasting an hour or two to adventurous voyages on live-aboard boats. Whilst trips can be thrilling experiences and can create lifelong memories, they vary considerably in both price and content. The best trips incorporate guides who can help you spot the animals and explain what they are doing. When guides are knowledgeable and well trained they can enhance the value of a trip beyond measure. Considerate boat driving is also an important factor. Dolphins respond very differently to a polite or an aggressive approach and good driving frequently means curious dolphins and prolonged views. However, we must be aware that any boat activity on the water, however respectful, is likely to constitute some disturbance to the animals, particularly so when dolphin watching often centers on the areas most regularly used and therefore probably most important to them. Arguments such as, 'If I were disturbing the dolphins, they would have gone somewhere else' reveal a fundamental oversimplification of the varied nature of the sea. The dolphins may rely on a particular feature such as an unusual tidal eddy or area of calm water. If this is crucial to their feeding success or the rearing of calves they might suffer a lot of disturbance before searching for a new home. In such a situation it is easy to blame the boat operators, but the market is driven by the needs and wishes of the dolphin-watchers themselves. If they were to demand high standards and considerate driving then the operators, who are usually commercial companies, would comply. So if you wish to watch dolphins from a boat, you can make the difference. Try and pick a recommended charter, ask if there are local guidelines for boat conduct and ask if there are trained guides on board. Most importantly if you feel that the boat is harassing the animals or you want to leave them alone then don't be afraid to say so.

If you are going on a trip it is always a good investment to be well prepared. Take a pair of binoculars (lower magnifications are better for scanning a huge expanse of water), waterproof and warm clothing, suntan lotion, Polaroid sunglasses, a dry bag for your stuff and sea-sickness pills if you are likely to need them. Bird and cetacean identification books may also come in handy.

Many people that see dolphins in the wild also want to photograph them and dolphin-watching boats are always made obvious from a distance by the glint of camera lenses. But like any photographic subject, dolphins present their own challenges. My first attempt took place on a commercial whale-watching cruise. The conditions were perfect: calm seas, minke whales, humpback whales and white-sided dolphins. I viewed the entire trip through the camera's viewfinder and could hardly wait to get the award-winning pictures back from the developer. Needless to say, there were no requests from publishers tucked in with my snaps. The learning curve for photographing wild cetaceans at sea is a steep one, but there are some simple measures that can make big differences to your pictures. The three main problems in photographing them from the surface are their speed, unpredictability and size.

Speed: dolphins surface quickly. A large bottlenose dolphin may spend less than two seconds at the surface and a pan-tropical spotted dolphin a fraction of a second. You must be ready so holding the camera near your eye eliminates the need to fumble with it. A little practice beforehand at getting the lens to point directly at an appearing subject makes a big difference. Don't be afraid to take lots of pictures, all professional photographers do. Getting the image sharp requires good focusing and high shutter speeds. Autofocus cameras make this job easier and prefocusing the camera on a spot where you think an animal will next appear reduces the camera's work at the vital moment. Shutter speeds are also critical, and a good rule of thumb for dolphins is to keep exposures shorter than a five-hundredth of a second. Strong light, fast lenses or fast films help.

Unpredictability: in most seas, when dolphins dive they vanish from sight. They may seem to pop up anywhere, but there is often a pattern to their movements. They may be traveling in a straight line, diving in a regular sequence or raising their flukes before long dives. Tuning in to their behavior gives you time to change films, wipe the camera lens or change position without curses. Keeping a good look out behind or to the side of where everybody else is looking often pays off.

Size: unless they come close to you, dolphins are always small in a big sea. Using lenses with long focal lengths (200-300 mm) can do much to bring the animals closer. If they remain small in your frame look for other opportunities. If you take a step back from the crowd leaning over the guard rails and frame them, the boat and the dolphins together you will come home with interesting pictures. Finally, I am convinced that Murphy's law applies to dolphins. The re-winding of a finished film always sets them leaping and cavorting. If you are near the end of a film and have another, then change it when nothing much is happening. If you don't have another roll, then keep a few frames spare just in case someone else's camera begins to re-wind!

For many people their first experiences with dolphins occur with animals kept in dolphinaria and marine parks. These animals and their keepers have done much to elevate the public's perception and affection for dolphins as well as providing many of the insights into their biology that we now have. Furthermore, the knowledge about husbandry that has been gained may become crucial in the battle to save some of the most endangered dolphin species. But our affection for dolphins has grown to such an extent that many feel that keeping them captive is no longer justifiable. Like most long-running debates, the 'should dolphins be kept for display, research and commercial benefit' debate is a complicated one that is clouded by personalities, falsehoods and the variety of conditions in establishments in which they are kept. To most people, squalid, cramped and purely commercial operations are unpalatable, while those that put the animals first, enrich their lives, facilitate research, promote education and use rehabilitated or captive-born individuals are more acceptable. To some, any sort of captivity is all right and to others any sort is too much. In the end, public opinion will prevail and as we are the public, the choice is there for us to make.

Seeing dolphins is one thing, but many people want to help

*Surf's up! Contrary to the popular perception, dolphins often come close to shore.
Like these bottlenose dolphins, they may surf waves crashing onto the beach, forage in the shallow
creeks and tidal bays or chase fish up onto mud banks. With a little detective work and patience, thrilling
views of dolphins going about their normal business are possible from the land. And the great thing is,
you can peek into the lives of these charismatic and wild animals without disturbing them at all.*

them. There are numerous organizations devoted to improving the future for dolphins and whales. Indeed much of the world's research and political lobbying is directly funded by charitable donations. The contributions of these organizations to promoting actual change varies considerably and many of the most responsible focus their attentions on the less palatable but ultimately more significant issues. If you want to contribute your time or money to them, find out where their effort is going and be selective; there are plenty to choose from.

If there are three things that unite dolphin research projects world-wide they are a lack of resources, limited time and too many things to do. This situation opens up a gap for volunteers to become involved and make a significant contribution; crewing boats, assisting in the office and, of course, collecting data. These jobs may begin as mundane tasks but as skills develop, can progress to be both challenging and fulfilling. If you want to pursue a career in this field, giving active help is often a good way of getting to know some faces and names, finding out whether the work really suits you and of getting a reference at the end of it. Alternatively, there are many activity holidays where people can gain experience of research work while directly and financially aiding the projects. Even casual sightings of dolphins can be of benefit to scientific research, and there are several schemes which collect this information.

Another way to find out more about dolphins is to tap into the abundance of material that has been written about them. Wildlife magazines often carry articles and there are many books devoted to dolphins. Unfortunately, these vary greatly in quality from those that propagate urban myths and wishful thinking to those that stand on a thorough scientific foundation. Some of the better ones are given in the recommended reading section at the end of this book. But if you wish to get to the raw information from which the best books were drawn, it is worth delving into the scientific literature itself.

Scientists of all types communicate their findings to each other and to the wider world though a system of short publications called scientific papers. In 1997, over 120 were published concerning dolphins. Like legal documents, these are written in a stylized format which can make rather awkward reading at first, because the text is peppered with other people's names and years. Known as references, these indicate who proposed an original idea or carried out the work being referred to. In doing so, these open up a Pandora's box of other papers, so if you are interested in an aspect of, say, the bow-riding abilities of dolphins, a recent paper should give you the key to finding all or most of the other works on this subject. Each of these papers, unlike many books, has also been subjected to a quality control called peer review. That is, other experts in the field have scrutinized the work before it is published and should have eliminated any half-truths or poetic licence on the part of the author. Scientific papers contain the jewels of what we know about any aspect of science and are published by specialist journals of which there are many hundreds. Most are obscure but thankfully the journals that publish articles of the widest general interest are kept by many libraries and so are the easiest to access.

Finally, by living in a modern society, each one of us is already deeply involved with the wellbeing of dolphins whether we like it or not. Shamefully, for almost every wild population the sum of our impacts has so far been negative. It is still, mercifully, not too late to turn this situation around. If everyone that enjoyed and respected them were to take action, by getting directly involved, supporting conservation organizations, shopping selectively or showing those who manage our environment that they are being scrutinized, then future generations of these wondrous animals need not suffer the onslaughts that their predecessors have had to endure.

The challenge is there. Make your involvement positive!

Recommended Reading

There have been enough books, magazine articles and research papers written about dolphins and the other cetaceans to keep a keen student library-bound for ten years. Whilst much of this material is specialist there are many general books that summarize our knowledge of them and the issues that surround their conservation. Of the books, here are some of the best.

Whales and Dolphins, by Anthony Martin and a team of experts. Salamander Books Ltd, London, 1990. A comprehensive review of the cetaceans, illustrated throughout with photographs and drawings.

The Sierra Club Handbook of Whales and Dolphins, by Stephen Leatherwood and Randall Reeves. Sierra Club Books, San Francisco, 1983. An excellent field guide, ideal for the pocket.

The Conservation of Whales and Dolphins, edited by Mark P. Simmonds and Judith D. Hutchinson, John Wiley & sons, Chichester, 1996. A collection of essays that deal in-depth with the issues associated with cetacean conservation.

The Book of Dolphins by Mark Carwardine, Dragon's World Ltd, Surrey, 1996. A celebration of all aspects of oceanic and coastal dolphins, brought to life by the author's extensive travels.

Dolphin Days: The Life and Times of the Spinner Dolphin by Kenneth S. Norris. W.W. Norton & Co., Ltd, London, 1991. A beautifully written account of the lives of spinner dolphins, our impacts on their populations and the ingenious ways of studying them.

The Bottlenose Dolphin edited by Stephen Leatherwood and Randall Reeves, Academic Press, Inc, London, 1989. A collection of scientific essays by some of the leading researchers on this species.

Also in the WorldLife Library Series:
> *Whales* Hardback Special by Phil Clapham.
> *Bottlenose Dolphins* by Paul Thompson and Ben Wilson.
> *Blue Whales*, by John Calambokidis and Gretchen Steiger.
> *Beluga Whales*, by Tony Martin.
> *Humpback Whales*, by Phil Clapham.
> *Killer Whales*, by Sara and Jim Heimlich-Boran.
> *Sperm Whales*, by Jonathan Gordon.

Biographical Note

Ben Wilson, a marine zoologist, has been studying dolphins since 1990. His work has focused on a population of bottlenose dolphins living in the cold waters off northern Scotland. Hundreds of days at sea with these animals have given him a rare insight into their daily lives and revealed many unexpected aspects to their behavior. Ben has also joined other research groups working on dolphins and whales throughout Europe, North America and further afield in a combined effort to understand how human activities affect their lives. By advising local communities and governments, he has been heavily involved in efforts to conserve wild dolphins. Ben has co-authored *Bottlenose Dolphins*, in the WorldLife Library series. He holds a PhD in biology from the University of Aberdeen in Scotland.

Acknowledgments

To my family, in particular Thomas Reid Wilson, my grandfather, who took the brave step of selling the family business to follow his interests in science. His aptitude to foster the same curiosity in all those around him has done much to shape my own path. For their generous sharing of ideas and guidance I thank Phil Hammond, Paul Racey and Paul Thompson. Kate Grellier, Paul Jepson, Harry Ross, Michael Scott, Alison Smith and Iain Wilson all made valuable comments on the text. And finally, I thank the late 'Kess' the bottlenose dolphin. No day afloat in the inner Moray Firth was complete without an update on her movements or the antics of her calves.

The Classification
of Toothed Cetaceans

Suborder Odontoceti
(toothed whales)

Family Delphinidae
(true dolphins)

Genus *Stenella*
- Atlantic Spotted Dolphin
- Clymene Dolphin
- Pantropical Spotted Dolphin
- Spinner Dolphin
- Striped Dolphin

Genus *Lagenorhynchus*
- Atlantic White-Sided Dolphin
- Dusky Dolphin
- Hourglass Dolphin
- Pacific White-Sided Dolphin
- Peale's Dolphin
- White-Beaked Dolphin

Genus *Lagenodelphis* — Fraser's Dolphin
Genus *Delphinus* — Common Dolphin (perhaps several species)
Genus *Tursiops* — Bottlenose Dolphin (perhaps several species)

Genus *Cephalorhynchus*
- Chilean Dolphin
- Commerson's Dolphin
- Heaviside's Dolphin
- Hector's Dolphin

Genus *Sousa* — Humpback Dolphin (perhaps several species)
Genus *Lissodelphis*
- Northern Right Whale Dolphin
- Southern Right Whale Dolphin

Genus *Sotalia* — Tucuxi
Genus *Steno* — Rough-Toothed Dolphin
Genus *Grampus* — Risso's Dolphin
Genus *Peponocephala*, *Feresa*, *Pseudorca*, *Orcinus* and *Globicephala* — 6 species

Family Monodontidae

Genus *Orcaella* — Irrawaddy Dolphin
Genus *Monodon* and *Delphinapterus* — 2 species

Family Platanistidae
(true river dolphins)

Genus *Inia* — Boto
Genus *Lipotes* — Baiji
Genus *Platanista*
- Bhulan
- Susu

Genus *Pontoporia* — Franciscana

Family Physeteridae
(sperm whales)

Genus *Physeter* and *Kogia* — 3 species

Family Phocoenidae
(porpoises)

Genus *Phocoena*, *Phocoenoides* and *Neophocaena* — 6 species

Family Ziphiidae
(beaked whales)

Genus *Berardius*, *Hyperoodon* and *Mesoplodon* — 19 species

Common Name	Scientific Name	Body length: Average inches (cm) Maximum inches (cm)			Preferred Habitats	Geographical Range
		Adult Male	Adult Female	Newborn Calf		
FAMILY DELPHINIDAE						
Atlantic Spotted Dolphin	*Stenella frontalis*	83 (210) —	79 (201) 90 (229)	41 (104) —	Oceans and coasts	Tropical and subtropical Atlantic
Atlantic White-Sided Dolphin	*Lagenorhynchus acutus*	98 (250) 108 (275)	87 (224) 96 (243)	43 (110) —	Coasts	Temperate North Atlantic
Bottlenose Dolphin	*Tursiops sp.*	102 (258) 161 (410)	102 (260) 144 (367)	33-50 (84-126) —	Oceans to coasts	Tropical and temperate waters worldwide
Chilean Dolphin	*Cephalorhynchus eutropia*	— 65 (165)	— 67 (170)	— —	Coasts	Western S. America
Clymene Dolphin	*Stenella clymene*	73 (185) 78 (197)	— 74 (188)	— —	Oceans	Tropical and subtropical Atlantic
Commerson's Dolphin	*Cephalorhynchus commersonii*	51 (130) 76 (170)	53 (134) 69 (175)	29 (75) —	Coasts	Eastern S. America and Kerguelen Island
Common Dolphin	*Delphinus delphis*	78 (197) 102 (260)	74 (187) 91 (230)	31-35 (80-90) —	Oceans and coasts	Tropical and temperate waters world-wide
Dusky Dolphin	*Lagenorhynchus obscurus*	74 (188) 83 (211)	75 (191) 76 (193)	— —	Coasts	New Zealand, S. America, Southern Africa
Fraser's Dolphin	*Lagenodelphis hosei*	97 (247) 106 (268)	93 (235) 104 (264)	39 (100) —	Oceans	Tropical waters world-wide
Heaviside's Dolphin	*Cephalorhynchus heavisidii*	62 (158) 69 (174)	62 (158) —	33 (85) —	Coasts	West coast of S. America
Hector's Dolphin	*Cephalorhynchus hectori*	49 (125) 54 (138)	54 (137) 60 (153)	24-29 (60-75) —	Coasts	New Zealand
Hourglass Dolphin	*Lagenorhynchus cruciger*	64 (163) —	72 (183) —	— —	Oceans	Sub-Antarctic and Antarctic waters
Humpback Dolphin	*Sousa sp.*	89 (226) 110 (279)	85 (216) 98 (249)	39 (100) —	Coasts	East and west Africa, Asia and Austral-Asia
Northern Right Whale Dolphin	*Lissodelphis borealis*	104 (263) 105 (310)	85 (217) 90 (229)	38 (97) —	Oceans	Temperate North Pacific
Pacific White-Sided Dolphin	*Lagenorhynchus obliquidens*	75 (190) 92 (234)	76 (192) 93 (236)	— —	Oceans and coasts	Temperate North Pacific
Peale's Dolphin	*Lagenorhynchus australis*	— 85 (216)	— —	— —	Coasts	Southern S. America

Common Name	Scientific Name	Body length Average inches (cm) Maximum inches (cm)			Preferred Habitats	Geographical Range
		Adult Male	Adult Female	Newborn Calf		
Pantropical Spotted Dolphin	*Stenella attenuata*	83 (212) 101 (257)	79 (201) 96 (244)	32-35 (82-89) –	Oceans	Tropical and temperate waters world-wide
Risso's Dolphin	*Grampus griseus*	113 (288) 151 (383)	109 (276) 144 (366)	43-59 (110-150) –	Oceans	Tropical and temperate waters world-wide
Rough-Toothed Dolphin	*Steno bredanensis*	90 (230) 104 (265)	91 (232) 100 (255)	39 (100) –	Oceanic	Tropical and subtropical waters world-wide
Southern Right Whale Dolphin	*Lissodelphis peronii*	– 117 (297)	– 90 (230)	– –	Oceanic	Temperate southern oceans
Spinner Dolphin	*Stenella longirostris*	72 (184) 92 (235)	70 (178) 80 (204)	30 (77) –	Oceans	Tropical and subtropical waters world-wide
Striped Dolphin	*Stenella coeruleoalba*	90 (230) 101 (256)	86 (219) 98 (250)	39 (100) –	Oceans	Tropical and warm-temperate waters world-wide
Tucuxi (Rivers)	*Sotalia fluviatilis*	57 (146) 60 (152)	57 (145) 59 (149)	29 (75) –	Rivers	North-eastern S. America
(Coasts)		63 (160) 74 (187)	63 (160) 72 (182)	30 (77) –	Coasts	
White-Beaked Dolphin	*Lagenorhynchus albirostris*	102 (260) 124 (315)	102 (259) 120 (305)	49 (125) –	Coasts	Northern and subarctic North Atlantic

FAMILY PLATANISTIDAE

Common Name	Scientific Name	Adult Male	Adult Female	Newborn Calf	Preferred Habitats	Geographical Range
Baiji (Chinese River Dolphin)	*Lipotes vexillifer*	85 (217) 90 (229)	89 (227) 100 (253)	43 (110) –	Rivers	Yangtze River, China
Bhulan (Indus River Dolphin)	*Platanista minor*	78 (198) 83 (211)	86 (225) 99 (252)	44 (112) –	Rivers	Indus River, Pakistan
Boto (Amazon River Dolphin)	*Inia geoffrensis*	91 (232) 100 (255)	81 (205) 90 (228)	31 (79) –	Rivers	North East of S. America
Franciscana	*Pontoporia blainvillei*	52 (131) –	55 (140) –	30 (76)	Coasts	Eastern S. America
Susu (Ganges River Dolphin)	*Platanista gangetica*	78 (198) 83 (211)	86 (225) 99 (252)	44 (112) –	Rivers	Ganges, Brahmaputra and Meghna rivers in Asia

FAMILY MONODONTIDAE

Common Name	Scientific Name	Adult Male	Adult Female	Newborn Calf	Preferred Habitats	Geographical Range
Irrawaddy Dolphin	*Orcaella brevirostris*	87 (220) 108 (275)	83 (210) –	35 (86) –	Coasts and rivers	Tropical and subtropical Southeast Asia and northern Australia.

INDEX

*Entries in **bold** indicate pictures*